PENGUIN BOOKS

THE CHINA FANTASY

James Mann is author in residence at Johns Hopkins University's Paul H. Nitze School of Advanced International Studies. He is the author of the *New York Times* bestseller *Rise of the Vulcans: The History of Bush's War Cabinet* and two books about China: *About Face: A History of America's Curious Relationship with China, from Nixon to Clinton* and *Beijing Jeep*. He was previously a diplomatic correspondent and foreign affairs columnist for the *Los Angeles Times*, serving from 1984 to 1987 as Beijing bureau chief. He lives in Silver Spring, Maryland.

THE CHINA FANTASY

Why Capitalism Will Not
Bring Democracy to China

JAMES MANN

PENGUIN BOOKS

PENGUIN BOOKS

Published by the Penguin Group

Penguin Group (USA) Inc., 375 Hudson Street, New York, New York 10014, U.S.A.

Penguin Group (Canada), 90 Eglinton Avenue East, Suite 700, Toronto,
Ontario, Canada M4P 2Y3 (a division of Pearson Penguin Canada Inc.)

Penguin Books Ltd, 80 Strand, London WC2R 0RL, England

Penguin Ireland, 25 St Stephen's Green, Dublin 2, Ireland
(a division of Penguin Books Ltd)

Penguin Group (Australia), 250 Camberwell Road, Camberwell, Victoria 3124,
Australia (a division of Pearson Australia Group Pty Ltd)

Penguin Books India Pvt Ltd, 11 Community Centre, Panchsheel Park,
New Delhi – 110 017, India

Penguin Group (NZ), 67 Apollo Drive, Rosedale, North Shore 0632, New Zealand
(a division of Person New Zealand Ltd)

Penguin Books (South Africa) (Pty) Ltd, 24 Sturdee Avenue,
Rosebank, Johannesburg 2196, South Africa

Penguin Books Ltd, Registered Offices:
80 Strand, London WC2R 0RL, England

First published in the United States of America by Viking Penguin,
a member of Penguin Group (USA) Inc. 2007
Published in Penguin Books 2008

10 9 8 7 6 5 4 3 2 1

Copyright © James Mann, 2007
All rights reserved

ISBN 978-0-670-03825-1 (hc.)
ISBN 978-0-14-311292-1 (pbk.)
CIP data available

Printed in the United States of America
Set in Electra with Bodoni Bold • Designed by Sabrina Bowers

This book is dedicated

to the memory of

Mike Jendrzejczyk,

who understood that

ending political repression in China

is a cause for

both liberals and conservatives,

both Republicans and Democrats,

and everyone else

CONTENTS

INTRODUCTION: EUPHEMIZING CHINA   ix

CHAPTER ONE: THE THIRD SCENARIO   1

CHAPTER TWO: THE LEXICON OF DISMISSAL   29

CHAPTER THREE: THE STARBUCKS FALLACY   49

CHAPTER FOUR: THE P-FACTOR   69

CHAPTER FIVE: LET THE GAMES BEGIN   89

CONCLUSION: WHO'S INTEGRATING WHOM?   101

AFTERWORD   113

ACKNOWLEDGMENTS   125

NOTES   127

INDEX   135

INTRODUCTION:

EUPHEMIZING CHINA

This is not a book about China itself. It is about the China I have encountered outside of China. It is about the China of the elites, about the views of China that prevail in Washington and the other leading capitals of Europe and Asia and in corporate headquarters around the globe. It is about the language, images, hidden assumptions, and questionable logic that powerful people—politicians, business executives, scholars, and diplomats—use when they discuss modern-day China. Over many years, a collection of ideas, phrases, rationalizations, and doctrines has emerged, all of which serve to deflect attention from the persistence of China's one-party state and its repression of political dissent. One might think that the problems of China's political system would raise both moral questions and practical ones, but apparently they don't. The book seeks to explain why not, by scrutinizing the way our leaders think and talk about China.

■ ■ ■

Twenty years ago, after covering China as Beijing bureau chief for the *Los Angeles Times*, I returned to the newspaper's Washington bureau. Editors asked me what I might be interested in covering now that I was back in Washington. America and Asia, I replied. They acted as if I were crazy. That's not a full-time job, one editor told me; there's not enough to write about. It was late 1987, and back then virtually all of the U.S. State Department, Pentagon, and intelligence reporters in Washington were of necessity spending their time covering American policy toward the Soviet Union (then in the final years of the cold war) and the Middle East (then as now a mess).

No, really, I protested. Asia policy is worth covering in Washington. Honestly. I've been living in China, and believe me, every week, sometimes every day, something's coming out of Washington that is of great importance for Asia and its future. You just don't realize these things are happening, because none of America's biggest newspapers is writing about them. We're the *Los Angeles Times*, the biggest paper of the western United States, and we should cover China more and better than our competitors.

And so, with my newspaper's grudging assent, I began to follow Asia once again, particularly China, but from a different perspective—this time not as a foreign correspondent living in Beijing, but as a Washington story, an American story. I started in the usual way, by covering the institutions that make China policy— the State Department, the National Security Council, the Pentagon, and the CIA. I attended the obligatory congressional hearings. But I soon became interested in the larger question of how America develops its perceptions and ideas about China, and the newspaper allowed me the freedom to roam into these areas. I began to spend more time at the Washington think tanks, those peculiar institutions where some ideas are formulated and others are ignored when they don't serve the hidden financial or other interests that help determine the work of the think tanks. I ate too many lunches (usually catered sandwiches or tasteless chicken) listening to what people said about China at think tanks of various persuasions, from the liberal Brookings Institution and Carnegie Endowment for International Peace to the conservative American Enterprise Institute and Heritage Foundation and back again. I hung out at universities to get to know the academic China hands and their ideas. I began looking regularly at batches of newly declassified material about America and China and occasionally at old archives, too. I even sojourned a couple of times to the convention of the Association for Asian Studies, the annual academic gathering of scholars who specialize in Asia, to see what might happen there. (Answer: Not much. Many people schmooze and look for their next jobs, and a few brag about the ones they have.)

Meanwhile, history was breaking out everywhere. In 1989, China's Deng Xiaoping summoned the People's Liberation Army to Beijing and authorized it to use deadly force against Chinese citizens, thus bringing to a bloody end a nationwide wave of protests against the government. Later that year, when East German citizens staged comparable demonstrations, its government didn't shoot, because East German leaders, and, more important, Mikhail Gorbachev, refused to follow Deng Xiaoping's example. The Berlin Wall was torn down and the Soviet Union dissolved. A few years later, Britain transferred sovereignty of Hong Kong back to China.

At the newspaper, I wrote about these events and what they might mean for America and China. Eventually, I left daily journalism and went off to write books full-time, sometimes setting China aside while I focused on other subjects and other parts of the world. But I still kept an eye on my old, favorite subject. I've now observed American views of China during four administrations in Washington, five American presidential campaigns, and at least seven or eight U.S. wars and military interventions elsewhere in the world.

Over the past twenty years, China and the United States have been transformed, both separately and with each other. During the

1980s, China was viewed as America's geopolitical partner against the Soviet Union, a huge but backward nation in serious need of Western advice and assistance. Today, it is seen as an economic colossus and a potential future rival. Two decades ago, many in Washington believed that China's Communist Party leadership intended to transform the country's political system as well as its economic system. The Tiananmen crackdown shattered that illusion.

Despite all these changes, the underlying attitudes of the political, financial, and intellectual elites have in many ways remained constant over the past two decades. For their own different reasons, the U.S. government and American (or multinational) corporations have been eager to conduct as much business as possible with China. In order to do this, they have sought to minimize the core issues of repression of dissent and China's one-party political system. And so an elaborate idiom has been developed for talking about the world's most populous country while avoiding these inconvenient issues. The elitists' construct of China carries its own terminology, its own internal code, its own pet phrases ("integration," "engagement") and epithets ("provocative," "anti-China").

In America, for example, the denizens of this strange world of the China elites have their own distinctive traditions. Whenever there is a top-level meeting between the leaders of America and China, one can count on America's leading China scholars rushing to publish newspaper op-ed pieces explaining the extraordinary difficulties Chinese leaders face. In contrast, whenever the Chinese leadership carries out a new campaign of arresting dissidents or closing down newspapers, the China specialists seem to vanish from public view. They do not volunteer congressional testimony or op-ed pieces on such unpleasant subjects. If they condemn Chinese repression of dissent, it is only in private, to their families and friends, or in quiet academic settings.

Over the years, I became increasingly fascinated with the vocabulary of these elites as they talked about China. I wanted to examine what the assumptions were, where they came from, and what purposes or interests they served. This collection of essays is the product of my explorations in America's China. The book does not seek to describe in detail the conditions on the Chinese mainland itself. For that, I would refer readers to the work of the many excellent correspondents who are reporting in China today.

In some ways, the American formulations and ideas about China are typical of those elsewhere. Other countries confront many of the same questions in dealing with China and respond in the same ways, with the same clichés, the same rationalizations. The Europeans and Asians now rushing to do business in China try to convince themselves, just as the Americans do, that China is changing, that their trade and investment are helping to bring political liberalization to China.

The view of this book is that it's not so simple—that we should not assume China is headed for democracy or far-reaching political liberalization. China will probably, instead, retain a repressive one-party political system for a long time. In fact, such an outcome may not bother the American or European business and government leaders who deal regularly with China; it may indeed be just the China they want. But they rarely acknowledge that they would be content with a permanently repressive and undemocratic China, not in public or to large audiences, because doing so would undercut public support for their policies. Instead, they foster an elaborate set of illusions about China, centered on the belief that commerce will lead inevitably to political change and democracy. The purpose of this book is to explore those illusions and the words and ideas used to perpetuate them.

THE CHINA FANTASY

CHAPTER ONE

THE THIRD SCENARIO

Over the past fifteen years, the discussions about China in the United States and in many other countries have settled into a familiar pattern. Whenever someone voices alarm about events or developments in China, that person is offered a soothing response that urges a more "enlightened" understanding.

Some critics point to the repressive, undemocratic nature of China's one-party political system. Others, such as workers and labor union officials, protest the loss of jobs to China's low-wage factories. Western business executives warn about failing industries. Members of Congress decry the mounting trade deficits with China. Generals and admirals warn about the growing power and capabilities of the Chinese People's Liberation Army (PLA). In one way or another, all of them ask: Where is China headed? In response, they are usually greeted with some version of the Soothing Scenario. *Don't be shortsighted,* critics are told. *Keep your perspective. Things in China are headed in the right direction. Look at the remarkable changes on the streets. China's economy is thriving; the*

Chinese people are getting richer. The country's rapid economic growth will lead to far-reaching political change as well. Eventually, increasing trade and prosperity will bring liberalization and democracy to China.

The Soothing Scenario holds that China's economic development will lead inexorably to an opening of China's political system. While this is merely one of the possible outcomes one can envision for China's future, it is certainly the mainstream view of China in America today. The purveyors of the Soothing Scenario include leading academic experts on China, business executives who are eager to trade and invest in China, and the think tanks and other elite organizations that depend on corporate contributions for their funding.

The Soothing Scenario has become the professed view of American presidents, too, both Democrats and Republicans. Over the past decade, in order to win the nomination for the presidency in either of America's two major political parties, it has become virtually obligatory to offer the American people some version of the Soothing Scenario: One must say, or at least suggest, that economic development and trade are eventually going to bring democracy to China.

George W. Bush paid obeisance to the Soothing Scenario for China at the very start of his first presidential campaign. "The case for trade is not just monetary, but moral," Bush declared in one of his earliest foreign policy speeches in November 1999. "Economic freedom creates habits of liberty. And habits of liberty create expectations of democracy. . . . Trade freely with China, and time is on our side."[1]

In saying this, Bush was merely echoing the words of Bill Clinton. The Democratic president had told Chinese president Jiang Zemin at a 1997 press conference that "you're on the wrong side of history," implying that "history" by itself might open up China's political system. Earlier that year, Clinton had declared that the economic changes in China would help to "increase the spirit of liberty over time. . . . I just think it's inevitable, just as inevitably the Berlin Wall fell."[2]

Press coverage of the 2000 presidential campaign mentioned frequently that Bush had differed from Clinton and Vice President Al Gore by calling China a "strategic competitor." However, Bush's supposedly tough campaign rhetoric helped to obscure the more important fact that on the core issue of China's political future, and on the role of trade in determining that future, Bush agreed with the Democrats. He refused to let even a sliver of daylight emerge between himself and the Clinton administration. Both parties embraced the view that commerce with China will transform its one-party political system.

The American presidents' British counterpart, Prime Minister Tony Blair, also offered his own version of the Soothing Scenario. During a visit to Beijing in 2005, Blair proclaimed his view that "there is an unstoppable momentum" toward democracy in China.[3]

The Soothing Scenario requires that any time some contrary evidence emerges—that is, some crackdown or other acts of repression showing that China's political system is *not* changing—the significance of those events should be minimized. One can count on the fact that every few months or so, China's security apparatus will lock up at least a few political dissenters or intellectuals or journalists or religious adherents or others who defy the restrictions of the one-party state.

Take the calendar year 2005, for example. As it had in the past, China continued to arrest and detain political dissidents, Tibetan and Uighur activists, lawyers, citizen activists, journalists, and Internet pioneers. Other prominent Chinese were kept under house arrest (including former Communist Party secretary Zhao Ziyang, who died in January 2005 after more than fifteen years of house arrest; his top aide, Bao Tong, lived on, also still under house arrest). China's jails continued to hold tens of thousands of political prisoners, including five hundred for the crime of "counterrevolution," even though the offense has been repealed under Chinese law. The estimates of the number of people executed in China during 2005 ranged from five thousand to twelve thousand; the Chinese regime does not make the exact figure public.[4]

In some respects, 2005 was not just a typical year; instead, the situation got worse. In small towns and villages, those who sought to challenge the existing order were subjected to increasing violence, including beatings by hired thugs. Near the end of the year, police shot and killed at least three and perhaps as many as twenty protesters in a village in southern China, apparently the first use of deadly force against ordinary citizens since the Tiananmen crackdown of 1989. Meanwhile, Chinese authorities launched a new campaign to restrict nongovernmental organizations working in China.[5]

There are a variety of ways in which proponents of the Soothing Scenario explain away such untoward developments. The first is by simply ignoring them or treating them as old news. From 1989 through the early 1990s, arrests and detentions of political dissidents received widespread coverage in the news media of the United States and Europe. The clear thrust of the stories and accompanying commentaries in the West was that the Chinese repression was outrageous and that something should be done in response. These days, similar incidents are greeted with shrugs and resignation. Few in the West are willing to allow the continuing arrests and jailing of dissidents to jeopardize ongoing business with China.

During the early 1990s, the White House was willing to speak out in public for the release of specific named political dissidents and to make their continuing incarceration a central focus of American diplomacy with China. During the late 1990s, however, Clinton stopped doing so, and President George W. Bush has not resumed the practice—again following the China policies of his predecessor.

American officials have explained the policy change as merely a tactical one: They pointed out that whenever the White House called for the release of a particular dissident, the Chinese government used that individual as a bargaining chip, demanding ever greater concessions in exchange for freeing the person from jail. The United States did not want to embarrass Chinese leaders or push them in a corner, it was argued; one should seek the release of dissidents only through "quiet diplomacy." The result of this White House change from public to "quiet" diplomacy, however, has been that fewer Americans are aware of the continuing political repression in China and that the White House had a freer hand to do little or nothing about it.

Those who put forward a benign view of China realize they can't always ignore China's repression. Instead, they often employ a different formula. We can call this second approach Two Steps Forward, One Step Back. When news breaks that China has rounded up a group of intellectuals, the proponents of the Soothing Scenario may, from time to time, acknowledge and quietly deplore whatever China has just done. But they then go on to say that one should not draw broader conclusions about China and the nature of its political system from this one particular untoward event. This latest arrest, they say, was just one minor setback.

Over the past two decades, the same cliché has been used, over and over again, to explain away repression or the absence of political change in China. DEMOCRACY, CHINESE STYLE: 2 STEPS FORWARD, 1 STEP BACK, read one typical *New York Times* headline. The text of the story reported, however, that "even as leaders are embracing Western-style capitalism, political change is happening only in tiny steps. Efforts to force political change are often met with hostility."[6]

Sometimes, when China carries out a broad crackdown, it looks as if the more accurate description would be "one step forward, five steps back." But the "two steps forward, one step back" cliché does not countenance such retrogression. Thus, even unpleasant news about Chinese repression tends to be safely embedded in an assumption of progress, a soft, warm, gauzy wrapping of hopefulness.

Another way of explaining away the significance of a widely publicized arrest or crackdown is to argue that in the case at hand, the Chinese regime was "ill-advised" or that the leadership somehow "miscalculated." The suggestion is that if Chinese leaders had only known in advance that their actions would attract worldwide criticism, they would have changed their minds. Rarely is it acknowledged that the Chinese leadership did precisely what it intended, anticipating the international criticism in advance and deciding to ignore it. Rarely is it admitted that the detentions of the moment might be part of a broader and continuing pattern.

When the repression becomes too obvious and heavy-handed to explain away, the adherents of the Soothing Scenario hope for faded memories. At the time of Bill Clinton's visit to Beijing in 1998, the first such presidential visit since the Tiananmen Square crackdown nine years earlier, some of Clinton's aides explained that the trip was aimed in part at altering American perceptions of China. The officials explained that too many people in the United States associated China with the televised images of troops and tanks rushing into Beijing to eradicate the Tiananmen Square demonstrations in 1989. "Many Americans see Chinese tanks facing down student protesters when they think of China, and Clinton's trip is aimed at presenting diverse images of how quickly China is changing," one U.S. official told reporters.[7] No one explained exactly *why* those images from 1989 should be forgotten. Should Americans also seek to erase from their minds the image of Richard Nixon shaking hands with Mao Zedong, simply because the photograph was taken so long ago and China has changed so much since then?

The Soothing Scenario assumes that a few decades from now, China will remain just as economically powerful and vibrant as it is today, but also that it will have somehow succeeded in transforming its political system. How will it get from here to there?

China's political leadership is still a Leninist regime, run by a Communist Party governed, in hierarchical ascending circles, by a Central Committee, a Politburo, and a Standing Committee of the Politburo. (Those who defend the Chinese leadership like to point out that because of the changes of the past two decades, China is not really a Communist country anymore. In economic terms, that is true; but rarely do such defenders go on to acknowledge that China does continue to have a Leninist political system.)

Will China simply glide over from Leninism to democracy? Will it one day morph into an open political system? When, why, and how will the leaders of its one-party state be persuaded to give up the extraordinary power they now hold? On those questions, the proponents of the Soothing Scenario are vague.

■ ■ ■

Although the Soothing Scenario remains the dominant view of China's future, one can also detect, not infrequently, a contrary outlook. This alternative vision is sometimes put forward by those who question the wisdom of a close diplomatic and economic relationship with China. Let's call this second vision of China's future the Upheaval Scenario.

The Upheaval Scenario predicts that China is headed for some sort of disaster, such as an economic collapse or political disintegration, because it won't be able to maintain political stability while continuing on its current course. Proponents of the Upheaval Scenario invariably point to the numerous reports of political unrest in China these days—the proliferation of labor strikes, farmers' protests, riots over environmental degradation, and ethnic strife. Many of the believers in Upheaval also look at broader developments, such as the ever growing disparity between rich and poor or the continuing prevalence of corruption in China, and try to sketch out how these will, over time, lead to ever growing, uncontainable political unrest. Others in the Upheaval school warn

of ominous economic trends, such as the fragility of China's bank-
ing system. Things can't go on the way they are in China, say proponents of the Upheaval Scenario. Eventually, the current system
will be pushed to the breaking point.

From there, their predictions of China's future go off in different directions. Some believe that political upheaval will lead to
economic stagnation or decline. Others think that upheaval will
lead to a sudden, dramatic political change—to a revolution or
collapse of the regime or an assumption of power by the military.
Still others prophesy that China will fall apart as different parts of
the country develop in different ways. In the mid-1990s, China
scholar Gerald Segal argued that the growing disparity between
China's rich coastal regions and its poor hinterland raised the possibility of "a breakup of China, whether peaceful or otherwise."[8]

The Upheaval Scenario was encapsulated in a 2001 book
called The Coming Collapse of China by author Gordon G.
Chang. In it, he wrote: "Peer beneath the surface, and there is a
weak China, one that is in long-term decline and even on the verge
of collapse. The symptoms of decay are to be seen everywhere. . . .
One day, the central government will not be able to fight all those
who challenge it; there simply will be too many."[9]

Over the years, American officials have also worried about one
version or another of the Upheaval Scenario. They don't go so far
as to predict chaos or a collapse in China, but they do sometimes
contemplate the possibility of chaos—indeed, more than they usually admit in public. In the years immediately after the fall of the
Berlin Wall, for example, officials of the George H. W. Bush administration explained that they did not want China to fall apart at
a time when the administration was preoccupied by the upheavals
in Europe. So, too, during the late 1990s, at a time when Republicans were warning of growing Chinese strength, Clinton administration officials countered that Chinese weakness was also a threat
to American interests. "As we focus on the potential challenges
that a strong China could present to the United States in the fu-

ture, let us not forget the risks that could be posed by a weak China, beset by internal conflicts, social dislocation, criminal activity, and large-scale illegal emigration—a vast zone of instability in Asia," asserted Clinton's national security adviser, Samuel R. Berger.[10] In fact, one of the recurrent strands of American foreign policy for the past century has been to prevent China from falling apart. The idea dates back to Theodore Roosevelt, who said, speaking of China, that "it is to the advantage, and not to the disadvantage of other nations when any nation becomes stable and prosperous, able to keep the peace within its own borders, and strong enough not to invite aggression from without."[11]

There are, however, reasons to be skeptical about all the forecasts that China is about to collapse or disintegrate. China is a huge country, and it is particularly hard to draw conclusions about the political situation from what is happening in any one place or region. Labor strikes may spread through all of northeast China, or political demonstrations may sweep through many of its leading cities, yet such events may not determine the future direction of China. There will always be large numbers of regions that are unaffected.

Moreover, mainland China has a long history of managing to hold itself together. The country may be broken up or may split up for a time, as it did in the twentieth century during the Japanese invasion and during the Chinese civil war. But the Chinese mainland has always managed to reemerge as a distinct, unified political entity.[12] Predictions that China will fall apart run counter to this strong historical tradition.

The exaggerated fears that China is in chaos or is falling apart affect even its own leaders. In the historic 1972 meeting where Mao Zedong welcomed Richard Nixon to Beijing, Nixon told the Chinese leader that his writings had transformed the entire nation. Mao demurred. "I've only been able to change a few places in the vicinity of Beijing," he replied. Apart from his false modesty, Mao was also giving voice to the recurrent belief of Chinese leaders that the country is difficult to control. Nevertheless, those leaders do generally manage to exert their will and keep the country from falling apart. China often seems to be on the verge of disintegration, yet the Upheaval Scenario mistakes the appearances of chaos for the reality of China's underlying cohesion.

■ ■ ■

Most of the debates about China's future revolve around either the Soothing Scenario or the Upheaval Scenario. The optimists say China is obviously headed in the right direction and predict that China will become ever more open, politically as well as economically. The pessimists contend that China is headed for a period of turmoil or collapse.

Yet the possibilities for China's future are not confined to these two scenarios. There is, in fact, another possibility: a Third Scenario. It is one that few people talk about or think about these days, at least not in the United States.

It is this: What if China manages to continue on its current economic path, yet its political system does *not* change in any fundamental way? What if, twenty-five or thirty years from now, a wealthier, more powerful China continues to be run by a one-party regime that still represses organized political dissent much as it does today, while at the same time China is also open to the outside world and, indeed, is deeply intertwined with the rest of the world through trade, investment, and other economic ties? Everyone assumes that the Chinese political system is going to open up—but what if it doesn't? What if, in other words, China becomes fully integrated into the world's economy, yet it remains also entirely undemocratic?

Under this Third Scenario, China would not liberalize its political system in the way that the Soothing Scenario predicts; but neither would China descend into chaos, as the Upheaval Scenario predicts. If the regime were threatened by ever greater political unrest, it would respond with ever greater repression—by calling in the People's Armed Police or, as a last resort, the People's Liberation Army. The argument for doing so, of course, would be that political upheaval cannot be allowed to disturb the Chinese economy. The party leadership would simply invoke once again the same justifications it has put forward in the past when calling for an end to protests or organized dissent: "Unity and stability are the overarching themes for the country and the people's wishes . . . ," said the *People's Daily* in one typical commentary not long ago. "Resolving any such problems must be done in line with the laws and the maintenance of stability."[13]

To contemplate this Third Scenario, one does not have to assume that a quarter century from now China will still be run by the same Communist Party that holds power today. Perhaps the names and the language will change. The Chinese Communist Party could change its title to, say, the Reform Party, and its top leaders might call themselves the Leadership Council instead of the Politburo Standing Committee. (There is even precedent for doing so: At one point a few years ago, the Chinese Communist Party announced that its Propaganda Department would henceforth be called the Department of Publicity.)[14]

Nevertheless, one way or another, the essentials of the current political system would remain intact: There would be no significant political opposition, no freedom of the press, no elections beyond the local level. There would be an active security apparatus to forestall organized political dissent. In other words, China, while growing stronger and richer, wouldn't change its political system in any fundamental way. It would continue along the same political course it is on today.

Why do Americans believe that with advancing prosperity China will automatically come to have a political system like ours? Is it simply because the Chinese now eat at McDonald's and wear blue jeans? To make this assumption about China is to repeat the mistakes others have made in the past—that is, to think wrongly that the Chinese are inevitably becoming like us. "With God's help, we will lift Shanghai up and up until it is just like Kansas City," Senator Kenneth Wherry of Nebraska declared during the era of Chiang Kai-shek's Nationalist China.[15] Those absurd dreams ended in disappointment. So, too, in the early 1950s, Soviet leaders thought they were re-creating a Communist China that would be similar to the Soviet Union. They, too, were wrong.

■ ■ ■

When asked to explain why they are so certain China will follow the Soothing Scenario, proponents often point to the recent history of other countries in East Asia. In particular, they regularly cite the examples of Taiwan and South Korea. From the 1950s through the 1970s, both had authoritarian systems in which police and security officials regularly locked up political opponents of the regimes. Then, during the 1980s as rapid economic development brought increasing prosperity to Taiwan and South Korea, both countries opened up to democracy. And so, the logic goes, China will eventually follow the political path of Taiwan and South Korea.

There are two problems with this logic. First, China is a much bigger country than either Taiwan or South Korea. It includes vast, impoverished inland areas as well as coastal cities of the east. If China were confined exclusively to these coastal areas, such as Guangdong, the province abutting Hong Kong, one could easily imagine it following the path of Taiwan and South Korea. Certainly Shanghai, with its educated, sophisticated citizenry and intense interest in politics, is as ready for democracy as any city has ever been.

But large expanses of China are isolated—geographically, politically, and intellectually—from cities such as Shanghai. Outsiders who declare that China will follow the political evolution of

Taiwan and South Korea, based on their visits to eastern Chinese cities like Beijing and Shanghai, are roughly akin to foreigners who travel only to New York City and Boston and then come to the conclusion that the United States will behave like Western Europe.

There is also a second, more important way in which China is different from Taiwan and South Korea. When those two East Asian governments democratized in the 1980s, both were dependent on the United States for their military security. Indeed, direct American pressure played a crucial role in opening up both countries. In the case of South Korea, at a key moment in June 1987 when the country was engulfed by riots, the Reagan administration bluntly told President Chun Doo Hwan he should give way and hold elections. In the case of Taiwan, prominent Democratic members of the U.S. Congress took the lead, making plain to President Chiang Ching-kuo during the 1980s that his Kuomintang government was rapidly losing American support and that the only way to regain it was through democratic reforms.

China will never be as dependent on the United States for military protection as were South Korea and Taiwan. It is vastly less subject to American pressure or influence. As a result, there is no reason to believe it will automatically follow their political evolution.

■   ■   ■

Often, the argument that China will inevitably democratize is accompanied by suggestions that, after all, its political system is already changing. "China's politics are still heavily steered from above; that said, the society is far more open today than it was fifteen years ago at the time of the Tiananmen crackdown," writes Richard Haass, president of the Council on Foreign Relations.[16]

Let's examine Haass's statement further. In one sense, it is correct: On the surface, things certainly appear to be better than in 1989, because the People's Liberation Army is no longer opening fire on the streets of Beijing. But why is that? The main reason

Tiananmen Square remains so quiet today is that China's security apparatus goes to extraordinary lengths to make sure there will never again be large-scale demonstrations there to challenge the regime. These days, the police don't wait for protests in China's major cities to gather momentum; they stop them much earlier. China remains politically stable in part because the repression is speedier and more thorough now than it was in 1989.

Of course, China is transforming itself rapidly, in ways that are not related directly to politics. Each year, millions of tourists, thousands of journalists, and scores of presidents and prime ministers travel to China, and when they return home, virtually all of them talk excitedly about how China is changing. In fact, if one did a word association test for China today, the word *change* would probably rank at the top.

Yet it is important to keep in mind exactly what is changing in China and what is not. Yes, Chinese people dress differently now than in 1989, yet people can wear tank tops or Armani suits and still not live under a democratic system. Yes, Chinese kids can eat pizza and drink Coke, but doing so won't necessarily create a free press or an opposition political party.

"China's going to have a free press. Globalization will drive it," wrote Thomas L. Friedman eight years ago in his book *The Lexus and the Olive Tree*.[17] His argument was that the Chinese leadership will see the need to provide accurate, unrestricted financial information to maintain public faith in its stock markets and that this process will in turn lead to broader press freedom.

Friedman's glib confidence amounted to little more than a new way of saying that Shanghai is going to become like Kansas City. I think he is wrong. Even if the Chinese regime permits fully open coverage of financial news (and so far it has not done so), this does not mean it will do the same for information and opinions about politics, government, or the Communist Party leadership. Chinese leaders are entering the globalized economy as rapidly as possible while maintaining controls over the news media. So far, they have managed to achieve both objectives at once. Their policies and their overall success may endure for decades.

■ ■ ■

Visitors to China sometimes conclude that the political system must already be changing because during visits to cities like Beijing and Shanghai, they can now hear private criticisms of the government. We might call this the cabdriver phenomenon: An American tourist in China for a few days hops in a cab, and during the ride, the driver confides that he thinks former president Jiang Zemin is a *tubaozi*—a bumpkin—or that the current Chinese leadership is lousy because it doesn't do enough to help poor people. From the cabdriver's remark, the visitor concludes that freedom of speech has arrived in China.

Yet the whole point of the cabdriver's remark is that it is private speech. He cannot publish it in the *People's Daily* or say it on Chinese television. He also can't organize anything on the basis of this speech. He can't call a meeting in his neighborhood to see if anyone wants to form a new political party dedicated to helping the poor. The fact that he can volunteer his opinion inside his taxi certainly represents a change from the era of Mao Zedong, when the cabbie would have been terrified to say anything. Yet it certainly does not mean there is freedom of speech in China—not in the core meaning of free speech, which refers above all to the freedom to talk about political issues in public settings.

Twice over the past quarter century, new Chinese leaders have suggested at the time they came to power that they might be on the verge of encouraging a more open political system. At the end of 1978, as Deng Xiaoping was gaining control of the Chinese Communist Party, he permitted an outpouring of dissent at the Democracy Wall in Beijing. However, within months after he became China's undisputed leader, the wall posters were torn down and the leading dissenters were jailed. In similar fashion, when China's current president, Hu Jintao, was in the midst of a struggle for control of the party with his predecessor Jiang Zemin four years ago, Hu identified himself with the cause of liberalization, in this case by permitting open discussion of the spread of the disease SARS in China.

Again, once the interparty power struggle came to an end, so did talk of greater political freedom. The living symbol of this turnabout was Jiang Yanyong, the retired military physician who first exposed the SARS epidemic in China. In 2003, while Hu Jintao was trying to show that he would be a new and different sort of Communist Party leader, the doctor was treated as a national hero. A year later, once Hu was firmly in charge, the doctor was thrown into jail for weeks and then kept under house arrest for more than a half year for criticizing the bloody Tiananmen Square crackdown of 1989.[18]

Indeed, in some respects Chinese politics is no more open now than it was in the late 1980s. During the period from roughly 1984 to 1989, under the two Communist Party general secretaries Hu Yaobang and Zhao Ziyang, China gradually began to explore the idea of creating an independent press, or at least a critical one, and of giving its legislature, the National People's Congress, some independent authority to provide a check and balance on the power of the leadership. With the Tiananmen crackdown of 1989, these ideas were abandoned, and today they are barely in the exploration stage once again. So, too, back in the 1980s, the Chinese leadership had gradually begun to create independent factory managers and had begun to strip Communist Party officials of their authority in the workplace. Two decades later, the party has attempted to reassert its authority in the factories once again.

The one genuine change in China that does undoubtedly carry profound political implications has been the arrival of the Internet. It means that the boundaries of private speech, symbolized by our hypothetical Chinese cabdriver, can now be expanded to chat rooms with audiences of millions. Even more important, the

Internet means that Chinese authorities have lost their ability to keep information out of the country. When Taiwan has an election, the Chinese people can follow it, day by day, debating whether Ma Ying-jeou, the former mayor of Taipei, is handsome or not and whether President Chen Shui-bian means what he says or is merely pandering to his constituency. When crowds take to the streets for political protests in countries such as Ukraine or Georgia, that information often makes its way quickly into China.

Still, the Chinese security apparatus has become increasingly sophisticated in its ability to block Web sites on the Internet. Key phrases like "Tiananmen massacre" or "Falun Gong" or "Dalai Lama" or "Taiwan independence" attract immediate scrutiny. The continuing furor over the role of American companies (such as Cisco, Yahoo!, Google, and Microsoft) in cooperating with censorship or security monitoring has underscored the obvious point that the Internet in China is not free. Let's suppose that someone in China wants to organize a new political entity—a Green Party or an independent group to represent workers in the factories of southern China. If that person tries to post a notice of a meeting for that new organization on the Web, he or she will quickly find that the posting vanishes and that it has succeeded only in attracting a crowd of security officials.

So the question remains: Even if people in China now have the ability to receive information from the Internet, what can they do with it? Chinese people can keep close track of an election in Taiwan, but they can't have their own. They can't even hold a meeting of fifteen people to sign a petition proposing that China hold elections. They can follow demonstrations in the Ukraine, but they can't organize similar demonstrations inside China.

The Internet has indeed changed Chinese politics, but in a circumscribed way. It has carried China from an old era of clueless authoritarianism to a new era of aware authoritarianism. For nearly half a century, the Chinese Communist Party ruled a one-party state in which the Chinese public was often kept ignorant of unpleasant news. Now, with the Internet, China has entered a new era in which the Chinese Communist Party rules a one-party state in which the public is increasingly better informed yet still cannot challenge or oppose the leadership. The Leninist system remains intact.

■ ■ ■

In recent years, proponents of the Soothing Scenario have developed their favorite panaceas for attempting to help China gradually become more democratic, without in any way challenging or upsetting the existing authoritarian order. Among elites in the United States, two kinds of reforms in particular have become especially fashionable: village elections and supporting the rule of law.

The push for village elections dates back to the 1990s. The main proponent has been the Carter Center in Atlanta, the organization set up by former president Jimmy Carter (whose admirable commitment to human rights and democracy, as we shall see, did not extend to China in the same fashion it did to other countries). The effort has also been supported by the international arms of America's Democratic and Republican parties: the International Republican Institute and the National Democratic Institute.

The logic of village elections was simple enough: If you introduce elections to a few hundred people at a time in the villages, then over the long run the desire for democracy will spread to large political entities—to Chinese townships, counties, and perhaps eventually cities, provinces, or the entire nation.

China had, in fact, been experimenting with village elections since the 1980s, when the Communist Party under Deng Xiaoping abolished the rural communes set up under Mao Zedong. Without the communes, Chinese peasants began to stop paying taxes and to defy government orders. The Communist Party introduced village elections as a way of reasserting its control in the countryside.

The Chinese regime then began touting these village elections to demonstrate that the country was becoming more open and democratic. In the United States, the Carter Center embraced these village elections as the centerpiece of its work in China, sponsoring efforts to train election officials, educate voters, and observe elections.

The problem was that these elections at the village level are unique; they are conceptually and functionally distinct from other kinds of elections with larger numbers of people. The key to understanding this is to focus on the importance of organization. You can run for office in a single village on your own without any organizational support by going door-to-door, because everybody knows everybody else. However, once you try to have an election that covers three villages, you need an organization—that is, one representative for your campaign in village A, another in village B, a third in village C, and so on. In order to form an organization, it helps to put forth certain common goals or values so that you can persuade voters to choose your candidate instead of a rival.

Of course, another name for an organization that offers candidates for office and advances a platform of ideas is a political party. And forming a new political party is still illegal. The Chinese Communist Party wants no competitors. It does not want to encourage, or indeed allow, the development of any rival political organization, certainly not one that has its own representatives from one village to another. So while the Chinese leadership has been willing to permit village elections since the early 1990s, it has blocked any movement toward elections at larger levels of society.[19]

Elections are okay, in other words, as long as they stay small, remain unorganized, and don't create any organization that could challenge the party's rule.

In fact, one might even say that allowing village elections helps to strengthen the rule of the Chinese Communist Party, by giving outsiders the appearance that democracy is spreading across China when in fact the party remains as much in political control as it was before. In many instances, the only candidate for a village election is chosen by the Communist Party. In contested elections, the Communist Party candidate usually emerges on top. In some recent cases, village elections have led to bloodshed when local authorities have called in riot police or thugs to attack those who posed a challenge to their control.[20]

Within a few years after the Carter Center began supporting village elections, Carter himself began to express pessimism about how they were working out. On one visit to China in 2003, he cited figures showing that only 40 percent of China's villages were complying with the law mandating elections. On another visit, he admitted he was not optimistic that authorities would allow any elections at higher levels, such as the township. "I don't see the immediate prospect of it, no," he said.[21]

■   ■   ■

The second panacea put forward in recent years is the rule of law.

The idea is that China needs to understand the concepts and intellectual underpinnings of democracy: above all, that a country is governed by abstract principles rather than the orders or whim of an individual ruler or a political party. Even if China does not have a democratic system now, so the argument goes, outsiders can help create the conditions for democracy in the future by introducing such concepts as due process and equal protection of the law.

Thus, over the past two decades many talented and knowledgeable Americans have made visits to China on behalf of initiatives for the rule of law. Some of their efforts are genuinely helpful, and none of them is particularly harmful. But the cumulative result of these efforts has generally been to reinforce the existing state of affairs—that is, a China that is commercially engaged with the rest of the world yet also remains a one-party state.

On the one hand, the initiatives for rule of law in China appear to have made some progress when it comes to business disputes. The leadership knows that in order to continue to attract and retain foreign investment, it needs to show that there are courts, arbitration panels, or other mechanisms for resolving disputes about money.

On the other hand, there has been far less progress in other areas of the law, such as the criminal legislation used to prosecute political dissidents. Above all, there has been no progress toward creation of an independent judiciary. China's judges remain under the control of the Chinese Communist Party. That has not changed, and all the American rule-of-law initiatives put together do little to alter that fundamental problem.

In short, these initiatives on behalf of village elections and the rule of law in China have, in fact, a common denominator. They create the appearance of change, while leaving the fundamentals of China's political system undisturbed. It is conceivable to imagine China several decades from now with village elections and an ever more sophisticated system of laws, drafted with the best outside advice, and all used to reinforce the same authoritarian political system that the country has now.

■ ■ ■

Why should Americans worry about the Third Scenario? What difference does it make whether China, during the next twenty-five or fifty years, remains a repressive regime or becomes a viable democracy? Is it because, under the Third Scenario, China would turn into a military threat to the United States, as some Americans on the political Right frequently warn? Not really; that's not the main problem with a permanently authoritarian regime in China.

To be sure, the expansion of China's military power is a significant development. Throughout the past decade, the Chinese People's Liberation Army has been building or buying new ballistic and cruise missiles, submarines, warships, and fighter jets. No matter whose statistics one examines, China's defense budget has been increasing steadily. The PLA is acquiring more than enough power to intimidate the countries surrounding it in East Asia, some of them America's allies. "Current trends in China's military modernization could provide China with a force capable of prosecuting a range of military options in Asia—well beyond Taiwan—potentially posing a credible threat to modern militaries operating in the region," the Pentagon asserted in a report to Congress in 2005.

Over the past few years, Chinese leaders have sought to reassure the United States and other countries that China intends to rise to a position of world power in a different, more peaceful manner than, say, Germany in the late nineteenth century or Japan in the early twentieth century. "China will firmly adhere to the road of peaceful development," President Hu Jintao told an international conference in one typical speech,[22] and one of his top advisers has developed an entire theory of China's "peaceful rise." Some Americans with an optimistic view of China tend to give credence to such reassurances; others are more skeptical.

It does seem clear that at present, China is eager to avoid any military confrontation with the United States and seeks instead to concentrate on developing its economy. Yet this could well be merely a temporary strategy, aimed at delaying conflict with the United States while giving China the time it needs to develop a more powerful military. Who can say what dreams and ambitions Chinese leaders may harbor thirty years from now, once the country is richer and stronger?

History and a well-developed body of political theory show that established democracies rarely go to war with one another.[23] If this is true, then the United States has a clear stake, in national security terms, in whether China becomes an established democracy or not. If it does, the chances for a conflict between China and the United States would be greatly reduced.

One should keep this military buildup in perspective, however. The bottom line is that the Chinese People's Liberation Army remains far behind the massive military power of the United States;

and even if the Pentagon is subjected to tighter budget controls in the future (an unlikely prospect), China has no chance of catching up with the United States even a quarter century from now. If China follows the Third Scenario, this does not mean that America is destined for war with China. It is conceivable that the People's Republic of China (PRC) may continue down the path of political repression it has followed in the past, and yet will continue to avoid any actions that would lead to military conflict. Chinese leaders seem to have learned the lesson from the Soviet Union that they should avoid any direct, prolonged, cold war–style confrontation with the United States.

■ ■ ■

However, even though an authoritarian China may not be a military threat to the United States, there are many other, more important reasons we should care about its political future and the prospects for democracy there. The first and most obvious, of course, is for the 1.3 billion people of China themselves, who deserve the right to determine their own political future just as much as do the people of the United States, Western Europe, Japan, or India. China's economy has changed dramatically, but the country is still governed in an unrepresentative fashion by a Communist Party with a long, unsavory, violence-prone history, a love of its own privileges, and a weakness for corruption.

Occasionally, the counterargument is made that the Communist Party does still, through some loose and intangible process, represent and speak for the people of China. Taking one step further, visitors to China, eager to come up with sweeping generalizations, breezily assert that the people of China "don't want democracy." Of course, such stereotypes are discarded during those rare periods, such as the late 1980s, when the Chinese leadership allows people to engage in organized political activity. At such times, it is obvious that people in China are as eager for a voice in their country's political life as are people anywhere else in the world.

Moreover, the answer to this shibboleth about Chinese not wanting democracy is simple: Why not ask the Chinese people to cast ballots on the question of whether or not they want democracy? How else can we know what the Chinese people want? If the Chinese Communist Party believes it really acts and speaks for the people of China, why doesn't it demonstrate that fact by allowing the people to show their support in an open election? Undoubtedly, there are *some* people in China who don't want elections—those who are now in power and those others who depend on the current regime for privileges or economic favors.

Of equal importance, China's existing, undemocratic political system is deleterious, both for the country itself and for the rest of the world, because it is unstable. There is no established process for resolving high-level disputes within the Communist Party leadership, and such disputes have led to repeated political crises over the past half century. China's increasing prosperity raises new possibilities for top-level schisms within the Communist Party over money, resources, and economic policy. The ruling party, to its credit, was able to work out a relatively smooth and entirely nonviolent transfer of power in 2002–2003 from its former leader, Jiang Zemin, to his successor Hu Jintao. There are no guarantees under the existing system, however, that all successions will be so easy.

Above all, if the Third Scenario comes to pass, a long-term authoritarian regime in China would pose considerable problems for democratic values throughout the world. Pick a dictator anywhere on the globe, and you'll likely find these days that the Chinese regime is supporting him. China rewards Robert Mugabe, the thug who rules Zimbabwe, with an honorary degree. It has been the principal backer of the military regime in Burma (Myanmar), where Nobel Peace Prize winner Aung San Suu Kyi continues to be held under house arrest sixteen years after she and her supporters won the country's last open election. When Uzbekistan president

Islam Karimov ordered a murderous crackdown on demonstrators in 2005, American and European governments condemned him; China rushed in to shore him up. China forged extensive ties with the government of the Sudan while other nations were concluding that it had engaged in genocide.

China's support for these undemocratic regimes is not merely symbolic. China gives tangible assistance—military help to Burma, economic help to Zimbabwe. China also lent a hand in helping to suppress dissent; in 2005, it was reported to have supplied Mugabe with new surveillance equipment to crack down on Internet traffic and block dissident radio signals.[24] Most important of all, China gives what amounts to ideological sustenance to these dictatorships; it lends support to the idea that democracy is an alien Western concept, something imposed by Americans or Europeans.

If, over the next thirty years, China maintains its current political system, then its resolute hostility to democracy will have an impact in places like Egypt, Syria, and Saudi Arabia. A permanently authoritarian China could also undermine Russia's already diminishing commitment to democracy. In 1991, during the brief, failed coup attempt by Soviet Communist military and intelligence officials against Mikhail Gorbachev, China's official press gave warm and extensive coverage to the coup plotters, barely mentioned Boris Yeltsin or the democratic opposition in Moscow, and was left stunned and disappointed when the brief putsch failed.[25] Vladimir Putin's recent drive toward a more authoritarian system in Russia is more to China's liking.

■   ■   ■

These reasons for wanting a democratic China—for the Chinese people themselves and because of China's influence on other repressive regimes around the world—are by far the most important ones. There is also a third factor, one rooted in America's recent history: If China's political system stays a permanently repressive one-party state, that will mean that U.S. policy toward China since 1989 has been sold to the American people on the basis of a fraud—that is, on the false premise that trade and "engagement" with China would change China's political system.

The principal basis for American policy toward China from the time of Richard Nixon's opening in the early 1970s through 1989 was that the United States needed China's support in dealing with the Soviet Union. Even for a half year after China's Tiananmen Square crackdown of 1989, the Bush administration continued to view China through this same geopolitical lens. But after the fall of the Berlin Wall in November 1989, the cold war rationale vanished.

Since 1989, virtually every change in U.S. policy toward China has been justified to the American public on the basis that it would help to open up China's political system. Whenever a president, either Republican or Democratic, spoke of his policy of "engagement" with China, it was said to be a way of changing China. When the George H. W. Bush and Clinton administrations extended most-favored-nation trade benefits to China, they asserted that the trade would help to open up China. When the U.S. Congress voted to support China's entry into the World Trade Organization (WTO), once again congressional leaders justified their votes as a way of helping to bring political liberalization to China. Across the United States, factories have closed and millions of Americans have been put out of work as the result of our decision to keep our markets open to Chinese goods. Meanwhile, the American people have been informed repeatedly that the reasons for our policy were not merely economic—helping American companies that do business with or in China—but also political. Free trade was going to lead to political liberalization. It was going to open the way for China to become a pluralistic country in the fashion of, say, Mexico. "Just as NAFTA [the North American Free Trade Agreement] membership eroded the economic base of one-party rule in Mexico, WTO membership . . . can help do the same in China," Samuel R. Berger, President Clinton's national security adviser, asserted seven years ago.[26]

These political arguments were the ones that made the difference. Without the claim that trade would open up the Chinese political system, trade legislation would not have been enacted. One can look in vain for American presidents or congressional leaders who said, "It seems as if China's going to remain a deeply repressive country, but let's pass this trade bill anyway."

So if the Third Scenario comes to pass, if the ruling Chinese Communist Party remains hostile to dissent and organized political opposition for decades or more, the American public will have been deceived.

CHAPTER TWO

THE LEXICON
OF DISMISSAL

Over the past three decades, an extensive lexicon has been developed to stigmatize critics of the People's Republic of China. Anyone who believes strongly in a democratic China, anyone who bluntly criticizes the PRC for its repression of dissent, anyone who suggests that the political situation in China is not destined to change or that trade with China will not lead to democracy—any of these critics is likely to confront a barrage of epithets, catchwords, phrases, and concepts that attempt to isolate the speaker before his or her ideas can be examined seriously.

We might call this set of clichés the Lexicon of Dismissal. Sometimes the words originate with the Chinese government, which is always eager to deflect criticism of its conduct and its undemocratic system. Sometimes the phrases emerge inside the United States. Either way, these pet phrases crop up in virtually any American debate about China.

Let's run down this Lexicon of Dismissal in order to explore what the words mean and how they are often misused.

"CHINA BASHING," "CHINA BASHER": These have become the all-purpose labels, the ones most frequently employed to insulate those who criticize the repressive policies of the People's Republic of China. Indeed, virtually any criticism of the PRC these days is certain to be branded as "China bashing." The phrase suggests that the critic has no legitimate concerns but is motivated primarily by some personal need to attack China. And what is "China"? Usually, the criticisms in question are of the Chinese government or Communist Party, but the phrase *China bashing* suggests inaccurately that the criticisms are of the Chinese nation or people or culture.

To brand someone a China basher is often a way of avoiding the substantive questions raised by that person. Obviously, issues such as human rights and democracy in China, or trade and employment, or currency and exchange rates, are complex. Moreover, any full-scale exploration or debate of these larger issues might run up against the uncomfortable reality that the public tends to support democracy more than American elites or that the public believes in free trade less than the elites. It is easier, then, to reject a critic of the People's Republic of China as a China basher, which suggests that there is nothing more to discuss.

The "bashing" terminology did not originate with China. Rather, the word was carried over from the Japan debates of the 1980s in Washington, which produced the phrase *Japan bashing*. In that decade, there was, in fact, one famous incident that qualified as genuine Japan bashing: In the summer of 1987, several members of Congress staged a public event on Capitol Hill in which they took out sledgehammers and destroyed a Toshiba radio after Toshiba's parent corporation was found to have sold sensitive technology to the Soviet Union.[1] In that case, the members of Congress were, in fact, actually "bashing." Later on, however, the metaphors *Japan basher* and *Japan bashing* came to be applied indiscriminately to anyone who criticized the Japanese government or Japanese trade practices. During the 1990s, the comparable labels of "China bashing" and "China basher" began to be applied to critics of the Chinese government.

These phrases are overworked and often inaccurate, yet they are increasingly in vogue. Originally, for example, *The New York Times* used the phrase *China bashers* only inside quotation marks—thereby indicating that this was someone else's phrase, not that of the *Times*. But by 2005 the quotation marks began to disappear and the *Times* editorial page began to embrace the pejorative phrase on its own, thus suggesting that it was a legitimate epithet.[2]

Step back a minute and note the disparity here in the use of language: If someone happened to *disagree* with criticisms of the People's Republic of China, *The New York Times* would not (one hopes) seek to dismiss those views by resorting to epithets like "China stroking" or "panda hugging," because such loaded phrases would demean the editorial page and stand in the way of genuine debate. Why, then, is "China bashing" so readily applied?

"ANTI-CHINA," "ANTI-CHINESE": These phrases seem to have originated not in the United States, but with the Chinese government. When individuals criticize the policies of the People's Republic of China, the PRC labels them "anti-Chinese" or "anti-China." Over the years, the Dalai Lama has regularly been branded as "anti-China," as have proponents of democracy in China and Hong Kong and religious or cultlike organizations such as Falun Gong.

This is, of course, a blatant attempt to confuse the issue and to wrap the policies of China's Communist Party leadership in the cloak of nationalism. It is possible (I speak from personal experience here) to admire the Chinese people intensely and also to dislike the policies of the regime they have never chosen to represent them.

"COLD WAR MENTALITY": In recent years, a new phrase has emerged that is meant to dismiss critics of the People's Republic of China and its continuing repression by suggesting they are somehow lost in the past. They are said to be reflecting a "cold war mentality." The phrase has increasingly been used by Chinese leaders, including President Hu Jintao, but has also been picked up by some American commentators. "In America . . . a lot of people are intellectually handicapped by what might be called a residual Manichean, or postmodern cold-war mentality," wrote journalist Tom Plate in one column about China.[3]

The implication, of course, is that China is being treated in the same way that the United States dealt with the former Soviet Union. It is an absurd comparison. One can see this most clearly by looking at economics. The trade privileges first extended to China in 1980 have continued to the present day. In 2000, the United States made those privileges permanent and successfully led the way for China's entry into the World Trade Organization. The United States runs a trade deficit with China that is now over $200 billion a year. China's ability to sell goods in the United States is one of the driving forces behind its rapid economic growth.

Given the massive Chinese exports to the United States and the equally large U.S. investment in China, any effort to equate talk of U.S. policy toward China today with American policy toward the former Soviet Union remains fundamentally flawed. None of even the most hawkish members of the George W. Bush administration—such as Vice President Dick Cheney or Secretary of Defense Donald Rumsfeld—has ever talked about cutting off trade with China. That is quite a contrast to the cold war, when the attempts to restrict trade with the Soviets and undermine the Soviet economy were among the linchpins of American strategy. The Soviet Union was never a normal trading partner of the United States; China has been one for more than a quarter century.

Moreover, to anyone familiar with the history of the cold war and China's role in it, the idea of a cold war mentality is ironic. China was the principal *beneficiary* of American policy during the last two decades of the cold war. Quite a few of the policies, concepts, ideas, and assumptions about China that were embraced in the United States during that era still, to some extent, endure today. This was the real, historical "cold war mentality" on China, one that favored the PRC.

Starting with the Nixon administration, the United States eagerly courted China's support against the Soviet Union (and China similarly enlisted America's backing). Henry Kissinger referred to China as America's "tacit ally" in the cold war. As one part of its larger anti-Soviet strategy, the United States decided in 1979 to grant most-favored-nation trade benefits to China while continuing to deny these privileges to the Soviet Union—and these trade benefits helped make China what it is today. The clear thrust of American policy during those years was to minimize conflict with China wherever possible. So the real legacy of the cold war in the United States, in its final two decades, was a solicitousness toward the views of the Chinese government, not discrimination against it. And the legacy of that era persists today. One can find it in the instinctive hesitation that many American officials and scholars display about voicing public criticism of the Chinese government. One can see it in the rush by the U.S. government to smooth over conflict with China. One can detect it in the eagerness in Washington to engage in "strategic dialogue" with China, where the very phrase *strategic dialogue* evokes memories of the Kissinger era.

Finally, one can even find a few vestiges of this old cold war mentality, from time to time, in the news coverage of China and its relations with the United States. Look at the daily stories, and one occasionally finds the cliché that some action or other by the United States "is likely to anger China." When then secretary of state Colin Powell shook hands in Panama with Taiwanese president Chen Shui-bian, *The Washington Post* reported that this could "anger China." A *San Francisco Chronicle* editorial wondered what might happen when John Kamm, an activist working on human rights in China, got an award from the State Department: "Will a government award anger China . . . ?"[4] Such press coverage suggests that the Chinese government operates like an irritable, angry teenager, one whose temper may erupt at any moment.

This journalistic convention, too, dates back to the Nixon-Kissinger era, when Sino-American diplomacy was intensely personalized. Back then it was feared that any slight to the feelings of China's top leaders, on however marginal an issue, might derail the fledging new relationship between Washington and Beijing. There is no other country in the world where the American press coverage frets so nervously about the changing moods of the leaders—not even the Soviet Union at the height of the cold war.

In the end, the phrase *cold war mentality* is something of a verbal trick. The true historical anachronism is China's Leninist political system, and it is this repressive system that is the principal source of opposition to China in the United States. But the phrase *cold war mentality* wrongly suggests that *opposition* to Leninism is somehow out-of-date, rather than the Chinese political system itself.

"PROVOCATIVE": This epithet is most commonly applied to government actions that challenge or criticize the Chinese regime—although the actions of individuals are sometimes branded as "provocative," too.

The implication is that the actor has gone too far, is unwise, or is an extremist. Let's scrutinize the meaning a bit more closely. Literally, "provocative" means "liable to provoke or arouse." In talking about China, "provocative" means likely to anger the Chinese leadership. This is an inherently subjective standard; it is of course up to Chinese leaders to define what makes them angry. An action could conceivably be legal, just, wise, and well-founded yet still provocative. To describe some policy or action as "provocative" is either meaningless or, worse, based on the view that the Chinese government is personalized in nature and that what counts are its leaders' feelings.

Individuals who take "provocative" actions are usually branded with another derogatory label: They are **"TROUBLEMAKERS."** Taiwan's two most recent presidents, Chen Shui-bian and, before him, Lee Teng-hui, were both "troublemakers." The Dalai Lama is a "troublemaker," too. Once again, taken literally, this is a meaningless epithet. The Chinese government itself makes "trouble" from time to time—and, like other international troublemakers (including the United States), it might even occasionally be right to do so. Calling someone a "troublemaker" reduces international diplomacy to the level of kindergarten recess.

Whenever troublemakers take some action that the government of the People's Republic of China won't like, the China hands in the United States can be expected to use a third metaphor-cliché: The troublemakers are said to be **"PUSHING THE ENVELOPE."** Taiwan officials in particular are regularly said to be "pushing the envelope." The implication of this cliché is that someone is trying to overcome existing restraints, to break through to something new.

Indeed, this shopworn cliché does sometimes accurately describe the actions of Taiwan leaders such as President Chen Shui-bian and his predecessor Lee Teng-hui, who have repeatedly attempted to broaden the limits imposed upon them by the reality that most of the world has no diplomatic relations with Taiwan. It's noteworthy that Chinese leaders, too, sometimes try to get the United States to impose new limits on Taiwan, ones that have never been set down before. Yet in Washington's clichéd discourse, the PRC's actions are almost never described as "pushing the envelope." When China seeks a new American statement or communiqué concerning Taiwan, or asks for an American denunciation of terrorism in Xinjiang province, for some reason America's

China hands drop the envelope metaphor and instead resort to explaining why the United States should be careful not to "anger China."

"PEOPLE IN CHINA DON'T CARE ABOUT POLITICS. PEOPLE IN CHINA CARE JUST ABOUT MAKING MONEY": This is one of the canards put forward by American visitors to China (including tourists, foreign experts, and politicians). The suggestion is that those who call for democracy in China are somehow out of touch with the fundamental character of the Chinese people.

When you think about it, this is on its face a demeaning national stereotype, one with just as little validity as the equally sweeping and equally belittling old cliché that "the Chinese don't care about human life." Of course Chinese people care about politics—some more than others, as is the case in all other countries.

Anyone who has spent time in the People's Republic of China during those brief, occasional, and tragic periods when the Communist Party leadership permitted people to speak out relatively freely—during the Hundred Flowers campaign of 1956–1957, or during the Democracy Wall months of 1978–1979, or during the period leading up to the Tiananmen Square crackdown of 1989—can bear witness that many people in China care intensely about politics and would like to have a say in how their country should be run. "I could begin to see a China I scarcely imagined before," wrote John Fraser, the Canadian journalist who suddenly found himself in the midst of the brief opening of 1978–1979.[5] If during other periods people in China choose to avoid political activity and to tell visitors that they don't care about current events, this can be viewed as merely a response to the political climate in China. People are not eager to engage in organized political activity if it will cause their careers to suffer or lead them to be thrown in jail.

"IF WE TREAT CHINA AS A THREAT, IT WILL BECOME A THREAT":

Over the past couple of years, various versions of this line have begun to enter the Lexicon. "We must defend our interests, but if we reflexively treat the Chinese as a threat, we will answer our own question: They will become a threat," asserted columnist Robert J. Samuelson.[6]

In classic military terms, whether a country is considered a threat depends on two things: its capabilities and its intentions. As I explained in chapter 1, we should not assume that China will become a military threat to the United States, because America's own military capabilities remain so far beyond those of any other country. But this seemingly punchy aphorism, "If we treat China as a threat, it will become a threat," bears further scrutiny. The suggestion is that the reverse is also true—if we don't treat China as a threat, it won't become a threat. But there are all sorts of logical problems with this notion, because one can imagine other possibilities. How China develops its military doesn't depend entirely on the United States. Moreover, China may react in different ways to American actions: It's conceivable, for example, that if the United States were to treat China as a serious threat, this would dissuade China from becoming a threat.

To see the difficulties, let's turn things around. It seems evident that quite a few leaders at the top of the Chinese Communist Party have viewed the United States as a political "threat" ever since the huge crowds at Tiananmen Square began citing Western ideals in the crisis of 1989. So if China treats the United States as a political "threat," does that mean that in response we will become one? No. Who we are and what we do doesn't depend much on China's threat perceptions.

The "threat" aphorism is an updated variant of an earlier one, which had more logical coherence. Back in the mid-1990s, Harvard University professor Joseph Nye, who was then serving in the Clinton administration, came up with the line "If you treat China as an enemy, it will become an enemy." Whether someone or some country is an "enemy" is primarily a question of subjective definition, a state of mind; a country is an enemy if we say it is — so Nye's formulation made more sense. This is a distinction to keep in mind. A threat may not be an enemy, and an enemy may not be a threat.

"IDEOLOGICAL": Those in the United States who favor the promotion of human rights and democracy in China have, in recent years, been subjected to a new label: They are sometimes branded as "ideological." This is a curious usage, since originally "ideology" meant a comprehensive worldview like Marxism or Nazism, not simply a belief in democratic government or self-determination. Under this new definition, Woodrow Wilson was "ideological," as were Thomas Jefferson, Mahatma Gandhi, and Martin Luther King Jr.

Unfortunately, the cause of promoting democracy has been damaged and tarred as ideological because of the way in which the George W. Bush administration and its neoconservative supporters pursued a change of regime in Iraq. Bush settled upon democracy as the principal reason for the Iraq war only after the grounds initially cited for the war (that is, weapons of mass destruction and the supposed links between Saddam Hussein and al-Qaeda) were found to be baseless. The neoconservatives, meanwhile, embraced Wilsonian democratic ideals both before and after the Iraq war but linked these principles so closely to the use of military force and to American unilateralism that the result has been to weaken support for the promotion of democracy elsewhere in the world, such as in China.

To seek changes in a political system that eradicates all organized opposition is not "ideological" in the original sense; "idealis-
tic" would be a fairer and more accurate word. Yet in America's
current political lexicon, promoting democracy is increasingly
mislabeled as "ideological."

In the current idiom, it is interesting to note what is *not* branded
as ideological when it might well be: an unwavering commitment
to free trade. Those who argue that trade will lead inexorably to
democracy, or that all other priorities should be subservient to principles of economic efficiency, are every bit as doctrinaire as those
who favor democracy. Yet our current usage suggests that somehow
the proponents of free trade are by their very nature prudent and
sober, while those who favor democratic principles are out of
touch with reality. Actually, sometimes the reverse is true.

■ ■ ■

The continuing use of this Lexicon of Dismissal raises a broader
question: How can we explain the elaborate intellectual super-
structure that serves to circumvent public discussion of the lack of
democracy in the People's Republic of China? Why do so many of
America's leading scholars and intellectuals seem so remarkably
complacent about the continuing repression of organized dissent
in the world's most populous country? True, many of these scholars
can point to something they have written on the subject—but usually these criticisms are in passing, or in private, or to professional
colleagues. Condemn the PRC? Voice public outrage? Testify in
Congress or talk to the press? Only a few are willing to do so. Why?

The best starting place for examining the attitudes of scholars
toward China is to explore the tension between two seemingly
conflicting strains of thought in American relations with the PRC,
each of them employed often, but in different contexts, by leading
American specialists on China (the people who are commonly
called "China hands").

On the one hand, the China hands regularly suggest that the ties between Washington and Beijing are terribly delicate. We have often been warned that things could fall apart. When Harry Harding, one of America's leading China scholars, wrote an early history of modern U.S.-China relations, he gave his book the title *A Fragile Relationship*. Whenever any public dispute arises over China in Congress or in the American press, one or another of the China hands will warn his colleagues, "Hold on to your hats, we're in for a bumpy ride"—a metaphor that conveys well the China hands' view that criticism of the PRC is akin to a pothole or bad weather and that a principal goal of American policy toward China is to avoid controversy.

In this characterization, powerful forces are often said to be lined up in Washington, preparing to destroy America's relationship with the Chinese government. Take your pick on who these powerful forces might be, because the supposed malefactors change from year to year: human rights groups, partisan Democrats, partisan Republicans, the "Taiwan lobby," narrow-minded manufacturers, organized labor. In contrast, those who favor the existing policy of engagement toward Beijing like to depict themselves as isolated and politically weak.

Now, let's juxtapose the China hands' persistent sense of fragility with another separate and contrasting idea, also voiced by leading American sinologists: that United States policy toward China has remained essentially the same for the past thirty-five years, since the Nixon opening of the early 1970s. "For seven administrations, U.S. policy towards China has been remarkably stable and could be called 'hedged integration,'" wrote David M. Lampton, another prominent China scholar, in one recent essay.[7]

Lampton's assertion is not *entirely* correct; as we shall see in chapter 4, there have been occasional perturbations in American policy toward China from time to time. But his claim is, by and large, accurate. Over the past thirty-five years, the essentials of the

Nixon-Kissinger policy toward China have been perpetuated. And the proponents of that policy—whether we refer to it as "engagement," the phrase by which it is usually known, or "hedged integration," the phrase Lampton uses—are the dominant force in setting American policy toward China today.

Yet wait. If American policy seems so durable, as indeed it has been, then why is it also characterized as fragile? And why do the proponents of this policy characterize themselves as politically weak? During every administration, whether Democratic or Republican, the champions of "engagement" occupy most, if not all, of the top positions for China policy. At the working level of government, these pro-engagement forces almost always fill the key slots at the White House, the State Department, and the CIA, and they often do at the Pentagon, too. Most of the China scholars at American universities and think tanks also strongly support the idea of engagement, as do the chairmen and chief executives of most Fortune 500 companies.

In short, when it comes to China policy, the proponents of engagement rule the roost. Why, then, do they have such an exaggerated sense of vulnerability? How can we explain the seeming contradiction? To understand that, we have to look to the past half century of American history as the current generation of China hands has experienced it.

■ ■ ■

Any examination of the China hands has to start with the bitter legacy of McCarthyism. Mao Zedong and his Chinese Communist Party announced the founding of the People's Republic of China on October 1, 1949, after having triumphed in the civil war against Chiang Kai-shek's Kuomintang (Nationalist) regime. Chiang had received considerable American support, and in the wake of his defeat, an acrimonious debate arose in the United

States over the question "Who lost China?" In the early 1950s, Senator Joseph McCarthy launched his crusade against supposed Communist agents and other subversives inside the U.S. government.

During that decade, several of America's leading specialists on China were forced out of their jobs in the State Department. Those who had voiced sympathy for the Chinese Communists in the 1930s or 1940s were in jeopardy. Meanwhile, American relations with China were virtually nonexistent. The United States had no diplomatic relations with Beijing and indeed virtually no contact of any kind. American and Chinese officials met, mostly to glare at one another, at international conferences in Geneva and at occasional, brief meetings with one another in Warsaw. In academia, China was a narrow and embattled specialty.

Then things suddenly changed. In 1971, President Nixon announced that he had sent his national security adviser, Henry Kissinger, on a secret mission to China and that he himself would be traveling to Beijing the following year. By 1973, the United States opened up a liaison office (an unofficial diplomatic mission) in Beijing, and at the end of 1978, President Carter announced the establishment of formal diplomatic relations with China.

These developments revived the field of China studies inside the United States. It is virtually impossible now to conjure up the excitement and romance that accompanied the opening of China. Those who had been studying the PRC from outside—from Taiwan, or Hong Kong, or just from textbooks—could make trips to Beijing and Shanghai. These contacts were usually well controlled; indeed, the U.S. and China governments set up official organizations to arrange trips for scholars, scientists, and others. But from the standpoint of the scholars who had been frozen out for so long, these trips, despite the controls, were certainly better than no trips at all. Back in the United States, meanwhile, there were new job opportunities; the U.S. government began hiring China specialists once again. However, no one knew for how long all these changes would last. In these early stages, the new relationship between the United States and China was, indeed, "fragile."

Such was the climate for young graduate students in the field of China studies in the 1970s. And the China specialists who were in graduate schools then occupy senior positions in the field today. Those who were between the ages of twenty and thirty when Nixon went to China in 1972 are between the ages of fifty-five and sixty-five in the year 2007. They came of age during an era when America's new relationship with China was exciting—but also when the memories of McCarthyism, with all its ugliness, were still fresh. They were imbued with a sense that at any point, on any day, some demagogue, some new congressional hearing, could cause America and China to return to the freeze of the 1950s.

This never happened, of course. For decades, the China hands proceeded through their careers without impediment. Indeed, some of them became so well established and so closely linked to American policy that they moved back and forth between academia and the U.S. government. But they continued always to be wary of a new return to McCarthyism. Hence, any upsurge in criticism of the Chinese regime, particularly in Congress or in the news media, was viewed as potentially threatening. China policy should be carried out quietly and left as much as possible in the hands of the executive branch of government.

It is against this background that we can examine the unfolding series of rationalizations put forward by American intellectuals over the past decades to explain away the continuing suppression of political dissent by the Chinese regime. The American public is, on the whole, strongly against political repression, and Congress tends to echo public opinion much more closely than does, say, the State Department or the National Security Council. As a result, whenever China's Communist Party leaders throw their opponents in jail or proclaim yet again that they are and will be the only permissible political force in China, such recurrent reminders of the nature of the Chinese system are somewhat awkward for America's China hands. They raise the fear, the old specter, that Congress and American public opinion might become too aroused about China.

Thus, over the years China hands have offered a series of explanations. At first, it was suggested that Mao Zedong's regime really did reflect the overall wishes of the Chinese people, even if there were no elections to substantiate this claim. China was said to be different, in cultural terms, from the West; there was no need for the formalities of voting or ballots or polling stations.

In the early 1980s, after Mao had died and Deng Xiaoping took control of the Chinese Communist Party, America's China hands began to suggest that Deng intended to liberalize the Chinese political system. Deng was, in fact, radically overhauling the Chinese economy; and inside the United States, some China experts voiced the belief that he intended to carry out extensive political reforms along with the economic reforms.[8]

These beliefs were shattered in 1989 when Deng dispatched the People's Liberation Army to shoot its way into downtown Beijing, ending the protest demonstrations that had brought up to a million people into Tiananmen Square. In the weeks and months following the crackdown, a few of America's China experts changed their views on how to deal with the regime.[9] Many others, however, kept their condemnations to a minimum and instead quickly devoted their energies to preserving the status quo, particularly the ties to China forged in the 1970s.

It was no longer plausible to argue that the Chinese regime enjoyed public support. Deng, it turned out, was not in favor of political liberalization. The brutally undemocratic nature of the regime was plain for all to see. Meanwhile, the events of the late 1980s in countries nearby China, such as South Korea and the Philippines, demonstrated that democracy was not merely a Western construct, but one that suited East Asia, too.

So after 1989, the shibboleth that the Chinese Communist

Party embodied the wishes of the Chinese people was destroyed. And so was the hope that the Communist Party was on the verge of introducing political changes. What to do? It took a couple of years, but eventually the solution emerged. The argument went like this: Even if China's regime was deeply repressive, and even if there was no evidence the regime had any intention of altering the political system anytime soon, democracy would have to come to China anyway. Trade and advancing prosperity would work together to bring about dramatic political change, even if the Chinese leadership didn't want it or was opposed to it.

The beauty of this argument, from the proponents' point of view, was that it couldn't be refuted quite as easily as the earlier ones. If you say that China's Communist regime embodies popular sentiments, then sooner or later an embarrassing incident like the Tiananmen crackdown will prove you wrong. And if you theorize that the current Chinese leadership intends to introduce democracy, then you may persuade a few people to wait and see for a while, but eventually, after a few years, even the most credulous listeners may ask why Chinese leaders continue to prohibit any organized political opposition.

However, if you claim that democracy will come inexorably to China someday, far off in the future, through the workings of broad historical forces and the magic of trade, then you are off the hook. The reality of continuing repression today doesn't undercut your argument, because under your theory the actions and intentions of Chinese leaders are irrelevant. Democracy—so the theory goes—will just arrive in some decade or another, with or without the support of the leadership. Better yet, no one outside China needs to do anything or even think much about the subject. Why bother to protest a crackdown or urge China to allow political opposition if you know that democracy's coming anyway by the inexorable laws of history?

This last argument, that democracy must come eventually to China no matter what its leaders do or want, is, of course, the

Soothing Scenario. With it, the China hands finally have a formula that enables the United States to conduct its relations with the People's Republic of China without worrying too much about its lack of democracy; the political system is going to change no matter what we do. Everything is going to be fine in the long run. For now, the best thing we can do is keep on trading with China, because trade will lead someday to democracy. This is the religion that has guided American policy toward China for most of the past fifteen years.

■ ■ ■

On February 22, 2000, *The Washington Post* published on its front page an interesting China story that then took on a life of its own. The *Post* reported on a Washington entity called the Blue Team, described as "a loose alliance of members of congress, congressional staff, think tank fellows, Republican political operatives, conservative journalists, lobbyists for Taiwan, former intelligence officers and a handful of academics, all united in the view that a rising China poses great risks to America's vital interests."[10]

The *Post* story was accurate. There was in fact a loose alliance of security hawks warning about China. Some of its members did engage in extravagant hyperbole about the degree to which the United States was threatened by China and did seek to tar or label with epithets like "panda hugger" those who disagreed with them. And some of these hawks did, in a burst of self-aggrandizement, refer to themselves as the Blue Team.

Yet the designation of a "team" was somewhat misleading. The *Post* story also acknowledged that the group was less organized than the phrase suggested. The supposed "team" had no membership cards or formal meetings; some of its supposed members disagreed intensely with others. But such nuances were lost in subsequent discussions, and over the following months and years, commentators in both the United States and Asia spoke of the Blue Team as though it were a single, organized, conspiratorial entity.

The intense public focus on the Blue Team usually left out the rest of the story—that is, the group of people working on the other side of these same China issues, seeking to avoid conflict with the PRC. They, too, were, in the words of the *Post* story, a "loose alliance" of members of Congress, congressional staff, think tank fellows, academics, lobbyists for the PRC, and executives or lawyers for the American multinational companies doing business in or with the PRC. They, too, tended to work together, to consult one another, to exchange plans and strategy, to talk to one another on a daily basis through their own small e-mail networks.

The braggarts of the Blue Team dubbed this rival group of China specialists the Red Team. This, too, was an exaggeration: The Red Team was not an organized conspiracy, either. Yet the continuing tragedy of America's inability to deal with China lay in the endless maneuverings of these two rival camps. Each group felt, with more than a little self-pity, that its forces were weak, disorganized, and helpless in the face of the overwhelming power of its opposition.

The polarization was so great that any new event or new issue concerning China quickly evolved in Washington into a poisonous dispute between the two sides. Members of the Blue Team not infrequently accused their opponents of being tools of Beijing or "panda huggers"; members of the Red Team called their opponents "China bashers." In the midst of this name-calling and factionalism, it was often hard for Washington to come to grips with China itself.

CHAPTER THREE

THE STARBUCKS FALLACY

A few years ago, *New York Times* columnist Nicholas D. Kristof gave voice to one of the most common American misconceptions about China's political future. It was June 2004, the fifteenth anniversary of the Tiananmen massacre, and Kristof was reflecting on how China had progressed and where it was headed.

The hard-liners within the Chinese Communist Party leadership who supported the use of force by the People's Liberation Army in 1989 had been right about one thing, Kristof asserted—that Western investment in China would bring a desire for "bourgeois" democratic freedom in China. "They [hard-liners] knew that after the Chinese could watch Eddie Murphy, wear tight pink dresses and struggle over what to order at Starbucks, the revolution was finished. No middle class is content with more choices of coffees than of candidates on a ballot."[1]

In one sense, this was merely another version of the same McDonald's triumphalism described in chapter 1: Once people are eating at McDonald's or wearing clothes from the Gap, American writers rush to proclaim that they are becoming like us and that their political system is therefore becoming like ours. Yet Kristof's words are also worth examining further, because they offer a window into our hidden, questionable assumptions about the Chinese middle class.

"No middle class is content with more choices of coffees than of candidates on a ballot." Here Kristof was trying to say something he thought was obvious, based on recent history elsewhere: Once Chinese people get enough money to spend on consumer goods and the other attributes of middle-class life, they will sooner or later push for a democratic political system.

But will they? Will the newly enriched, Starbucks-sipping, apartment-buying, car-driving denizens of China's largest cities in fact become the vanguard for democracy in China? Or is it possible that China's middle-class elite will either fail to embrace calls for a democratic China or even turn out to be a driving force in *opposition* to democracy?

The story line that Americans envision for China's future has a very simple logic. It goes like this: (1) China is now run by the Communist Party. (2) China has an emerging middle class. (3) Eventually, these two forces will collide with each other, and the middle class will force the Communist Party to give way to democracy.

For China, however, such a narrative amounts to a fantasy, one that leaves out many complexities. It omits mention, for example, of China's rural peasants, its urban workers, and the tens of millions of migrants now living in Chinese cities. And it also overlooks the critical impact that these other groups within Chinese society may have on China's middle class and its attitudes toward democracy.

■ ■ ■

To see this, let's go back once more to that comparison with neighboring countries in East Asia. In his column, Kristof embraced the conventional wisdom that democracy will come to China "in roughly the same way that democracy infiltrated South Korea and Taiwan."[2]

As we have seen in chapter 1, however, South Korea and Taiwan differ from China in several respects. China does not depend for its security upon the United States, which at crucial moments during the 1980s pressed hard for an opening to democracy in both Taiwan and South Korea. Moreover, China is geographically much larger than Taiwan and South Korea; it has a vast interior that is not tied to the intellectual and political trends of the East Asian coastal areas.

There is also one more way in which China is different from South Korea or Taiwan, and it is a factor of profound importance for any consideration of how China's middle class will react to the idea of democracy. China's emerging urban middle class is merely a tiny proportion of the country's overall population—far smaller than in Taiwan or South Korea. There are an estimated 800 million to 900 million Chinese peasants—most of them living in rural areas, although 100 million or more are working or trying to find jobs as migrants on the margins of Chinese cities.

The old rural-urban ratio for China, in the era of Mao Zedong, was roughly four to one: four peasants in the countryside for every one urban resident. Now that rural-urban ratio is significantly less, roughly two to one, primarily because of the movement of peasants to the cities. But the underlying significance of this huge imbalance is still the same: If China were to have nationwide elections, and if peasants were to vote their own interests, separate from those of the Starbucks sippers in the cities, then the urban middle class would lose. The margin would not be close, like the red-state, blue-state divide of recent American elections. On an electoral map of China, the biggest cities like Shanghai, Beijing, Tianjin, and Guangzhou might look something like the small gold stars on the Chinese flag; they would be surrounded by a sea of red.

Add together the population of China's ten biggest cities—Shanghai, Beijing, Tianjin, Wuhan, Shenyang, Chongqing, Guangzhou, Chengdu, Xi'an, and Changchun—and you get a total of roughly 62 million people. That number is larger than the population of France or Britain or Italy. But for China, it is not much: It is still only 5 percent of China's overall population of 1.3 billion.

Thus the paradox: The emergence of China's urban middle class is far more significant for its size when measured against the rest of the world than it is as a proportion of China's overall population. If you are a multinational company trying to sell consumer products, such as soap or cars or deodorant, then the rapid rise in spendable income in China's largest cities is of staggering importance. Shanghai alone is a market comparable to Seoul, Taipei, or Tokyo, and there are many other Chinese cities behind it. However, the mathematics changes when we turn from marketing to democracy. When it comes to any national elections, that new Chinese middle class, the Starbucks clientele, is merely a drop in the bucket. Those in the avant-garde in Chinese cities have every reason to fear that in nationwide elections they would be outvoted.

This would be true enough based merely on the population statistics. In addition, China's urban residents have an even greater reason to fear democracy: The Chinese Communist Party has not exactly been evenhanded in its treatment of urban residents vis-à-vis peasants. On the contrary: Its policies have strongly favored the cities over the countryside. This was true even under Mao Zedong, when the regime made sure that bread and rice remained cheap in Chinese cities. And it has been increasingly true in the three decades since Mao's death. As China has switched from centralized planning to markets, opening up its economy to the outside world, and as the Chinese economy has responded with remarkable rates of growth, the urban residents are the ones who have gotten rich—or at least much richer than they were.

Those in the countryside have done not nearly so well. This is why there has been a wave of protests in the countryside, arising out of land seizures, local taxes, disputes over village elections, and similar controversies. And it is also why the Chinese regime has been, in recent years, particularly fearful of mass movements that might sweep through the countryside and undermine the Communist Party's control. Looking at Falun Gong, the quasi-religious movement that began to take hold during the 1990s, the Chinese leadership was haunted by a specter from the past: the Taiping rebellion that swept out of middle China in the nineteenth century and shook the Qing dynasty to its foundations.

Let's return now to Kristof's idea that the Chinese middle class is going to want multiple political candidates together with its choices at Starbucks. This might well prove accurate when it comes to elections for, say, a middle-class neighborhood like Beijing's upscale Haidian district or for the entire city of Shanghai. But it probably won't turn out to be true when the middle-class people contemplate the idea of elections to decide who will lead the nation. To protect their own economic interests, China's urban elite may opt for a one-party state over one man, one vote.

■ ■ ■

In order to understand China's future, we need to develop a more sophisticated understanding of what now keeps the Chinese political system going. What lies behind the Chinese Communist Party's monopoly on power and its continuing repression of dissent? The answer usually offered is the Communist Party itself. It is often said that the party and its 69 million members are clinging to their own power and privileges. This is certainly part of the answer, but not all of it. As China's economy has thrived in recent years, strong economic and social forces have also emerged in Chinese society that will seek to protect the existing order and their own economic interests. The new middle class in Chinese cities is coming to favor the status quo nearly as much as does the Communist Party itself.

This suggests that there may be two different scenarios for a nondemocratic future in China over the coming years. One is that the Communist Party will continue to hold on to power for another couple of decades, with the backing of the urban elite. The second scenario is that the Chinese Communist Party might give up power, or be forced to do so, but would be replaced by a successor regime that also refuses to allow dissent or political opposition.

Why do we assume that if the Communist Party someday falls from power in China, what follows would necessarily be political liberalization or democracy? One can envision other possibilities. Suppose, for example, the Chinese Communist Party proves over the next decade to be no better at combating the country's endemic corruption than it has been over the past decade. Finally, public revulsion over this corruption reaches the point where the Chinese people are ready to take to the streets. China's leaders threaten to call in the army but realize that they can't rely on the loyalty of either the officers or the troops; and so, sooner or later, the Communist Party gives way. Even then, would the result be Chinese democracy? Not necessarily. China's urban middle class might choose to align itself with the military and the security apparatus to support some other form of authoritarian regime, arguing that it is necessary to do so to keep the economy running.

■   ■   ■

Americans have frequently formed their views of China on the basis of limited or skewed information. In the early 1970s, at the time of Richard Nixon's opening, when the first groups of Americans began visiting China, they spent most of their time talking to Communist Party officials or the people they chose. These early American visitors had little choice; their trips to China were controlled and their appointments carefully restricted.

What the Americans saw and learned about China in those days, then, was based almost entirely on what Communist Party leaders wanted outsiders to believe. Some of their errors are now legendary.

During the Cultural Revolution, actress Shirley MacLaine was brought by party officials to talk to a Chinese nuclear scientist who had been sent out to the countryside. He told her that his work as a farm laborer growing tomatoes was as meaningful to him as learning how to split the atom. A few years later, she related this story to China's new leader, Deng Xiaoping, who told her, "He lied to you."[3]

Similarly, the predictions Americans made on these early trips to China often turned out to be wrong. On September 10, 1976, the day after Mao's death, the American author Orville Schell, who had been writing a book in China, wrote that Mao's legacy and revolutionary spirit would prove to be lasting. "I believe that . . . the political features of China and life for the average man will remain much as they were when I witnessed them," Schell asserted.[4] Within barely a few years, American writers, Schell among them, ably chronicled China's thorough rejection of Maoism.

These days, visitors are able to see much more of China. Americans are traveling to the country in numbers of close to a million a year. While China's Ministry of State Security may still keep watch in the background, the visitors to China nevertheless enjoy vastly greater freedom. Tourists can wander around China virtually as they please. American scholars talk regularly to Chinese scholars; business executives converse with, hire, and work alongside Chinese counterparts.

Yet despite all this increased contact and freedom of movement, the Americans come home from China with a picture of the country that is still skewed, although in a different way. The Americans spend most or all of their time in the biggest cities, not the rural areas; indeed, travelers to China often devote their trips to Beijing, Shanghai, and a handful of tourist designations such as Xi'an, Hangzhou, and Guilin. American scholars travel regularly to China, but their conferences and exchanges with their counterparts are usually in Beijing or Shanghai. Inevitably, most of the interactions Americans have in China are with government officials, scholars, investment advisers, business managers, and museum guides, not with garbage collectors, construction workers, or street sweepers.

Therefore, when Americans come home from vacations or business trips to China and make sweeping generalizations about the country or its people, the views they convey tend to be those of China's urban middle class. The returning Americans say that things are going swimmingly well for "China" or that the "Chinese" are getting rich, when they really mean the elites in the big cities. The returnees sometimes report that "the Chinese we talked to" think that democracy would lead to chaos or that it might damage the booming economy. But the Chinese whom the visitors see are not necessarily representative of the entire country; there are other Chinese in the countryside and in the migrant communities of Chinese cities who have little or no stake in the booming economy.

Ironically, in assuming that the urban elites represent China as a whole and in ignoring the rural areas, the United States is repeating a mistake it has made before. In the 1930s, Americans developed close ties to Chiang Kai-shek's Kuomintang (Nationalist) government and to the urban middle class that seemed to be thriving under its rule. In the process, the Americans failed to recognize how the Kuomintang's policies were failing in the countryside, stimulating the sorts of resentments among the peasantry that led to the Chinese revolution. Today, China's Communist Party, the vanguard of that revolution of the 1930s and 1940s, seems to be alienating rural China much as the Kuomintang did.

This does not mean that there will be a political revolution in the countryside once again, as there was sixty years ago. In fact, the likelihood is that China's current regime will be able to repress the dissent and protests, with the help of police and security forces. Rather, the point is that the visitors' generalizations about a glitzy, modernizing China usually overlook the many hundreds of millions of Chinese in the countryside whom the visitors have not met on their trips to Beijing and Shanghai. In the excitement at seeing skyscrapers, neon, fast food, and fashion, the visiting Americans form impressions of China that are focused almost entirely on the middle class and the elites.

■ ■ ■

For ordinary Americans, the inability to come to grips with China's one-party state is simply a matter of misperception: the illusions about the Taiwan–South Korea model for China, the overestimation of the role of the Chinese middle class. However, among America's intellectual, political, and financial leaders, the dynamics are more complex. One finds a strong reluctance to challenge the status quo in China and a willingness to ignore or explain away China's continuing repression. One also finds, not infrequently, a strong sympathy with China's leaders and their problems, despite the authoritarian nature of the system.

If you listen carefully to the public debate in the United States over China policy, you can sometimes detect a strain of thought that might be called the Embattled Elites Equivalence and Commiseration School. It goes like this:

> The good guys in America and the good guys in China have to team up to fight our opponents in both countries. . . . There are critics in the United States who want tougher policies toward China, and there are hawks in China who seek tougher policies toward America. Let's join together against them.

This is an unusual version of an "us against them" mentality. All persons, both Americans and Chinese, are classified in simple terms according to their views on Sino-American relations. If they are in favor of close relations between the two governments, then they are part of the same team. If not, and if they seek to challenge the existing order for whatever reason, then they are on the opposing team, no matter whether they are Americans or Chinese and no matter what their particular views might be.

Consider the following passage from a book by David M. Lampton, the American China scholar and former president of the National Committee for U.S.-China Relations:

> A *Chinese acquaintance, speaking about "America Firster" Patrick Buchanan and his PRC analogue, Deng Liqun, commented, "You Americans have your fundamentalists, and so do we."*[5]

His name is not well known in the United States, but Deng Liqun (no relation to Chinese leader Deng Xiaoping) was for years the Chinese Communist Party's most prominent proponent of old-school Marxist orthodoxy; he led several campaigns against Western or capitalist influences in China during the 1980s and 1990s. Buchanan has been a leading American isolationist and anti-Communist. These two men have almost entirely different and conflicting sets of beliefs. Yet in Lampton's schema they are "analogues," lumped together because they have both denounced (from opposite directions) the existing relationship between Washington and Beijing. The suggestion is that if someone opposes a close Sino-American partnership, that person is a "fundamentalist" or an extremist.

One corollary advanced in recent years by the Embattled Elites Equivalence and Commiseration School is the following canard: "Leaders in China must deal with public opinion in their country, just as American leaders do." This proposition starts with a kernel of truth: Public opinion is indeed a more significant factor in China than it used to be. Modern communications, including the Internet and cell phones, have made it easier to spread private opinions without going through the official press. Moreover, the Chinese Communist Party has at times resorted to stoking nationalist sentiments (against Japan or, less often, against the United States) to shore up support for the regime; and whenever it does this, it runs a risk that those nationalist sentiments will spin out of control.

The problem comes with the next step: the suggestion that Chinese and American leaders are in the same boat, because in both countries they have to deal with public opinion and with domestic opposition to their policies. This glosses over the fundamental difference between the two political systems, one democratic and the other still Leninist. The domestic opposition that China's leaders worry about comes from within the Communist Party or the People's Liberation Army; other opposition is not permitted to exist, at least not in any organized way. When Chinese public opinion becomes troublesome for China's top leaders, they can rein it in by blocking Web sites and banning public demonstrations—as the regime did in the spring of 2005 when a wave of anti-Japanese demonstrations ventured a bit further than the leadership wanted.

■ ■ ■

The proclivity of American elites to refrain from public criticism of China's repressive system is reinforced all the more by the influence of money. There are huge and growing financial incentives for prominent Americans to support the status quo in China (or to argue that the status quo need not be challenged, because trade and investment will somehow eventually make things better).

In Washington, U.S. political leaders and cabinet members know that if they become involved in dealing with China and don't become identified as critics of the regime in Beijing, when they leave office they can move on to lucrative careers as advisers, consultants, or hand-holders for corporate executives eager to do business in China. This is, of course, an old story; the career path was blazed long ago by Henry Kissinger, who after stepping down as secretary of state set up his own consulting firm, Kissinger Associates, and began escorting American bankers and other executives to Beijing.

Now, Kissinger stands out in his consulting work only because of the size of his fees. An ever increasing number of former U.S. officials have followed Kissinger's example. When the Clinton administration left office, National Security Adviser Samuel R. Berger set up a consulting firm, Stonebridge International, which gives advice and help on China in the fashion of Kissinger. Like Kissinger, Berger sojourns regularly to China, where he meets with Chinese officials and is identified as the former national security adviser; meanwhile, he is able to further the interests of his business clients. "I'm a consultant to government and to business, in the political and economic spheres," Berger told China's state-run Xinhua News Service on one of his trips. "My two identities are like two hats, but they both play the role of bridge in the development of U.S.-China relations."[6]

It would be unfair to single out Berger. After Clinton left office, his secretary of state, Madeleine K. Albright, formed the Albright Group, and his defense secretary, William S. Cohen, formed the Cohen Group. Both provide advice for companies eager to do business in China. Companies seeking China advice with a more Republican cast can turn to Hills & Co. (headed by former U.S. trade representative Carla A. Hills), the Scowcroft Group (former national security adviser Brent Scowcroft), or, of course, Kissinger Associates.[7]

Washington's leading law firms, meanwhile, also compete to recruit former cabinet members who have been involved in China policy and can claim, like Berger, to have the "two hats" of government and private business. During Clinton's first term, Mickey Kantor served as U.S. trade representative and commerce secretary, negotiating a series of intellectual property disputes with

China. Then he went off to a private law firm, Mayer, Brown, Rowe & Maw, taking with him the two top China specialists from the Office of the U.S. Trade Representative. Kantor's successor at the USTR, Charlene Barshefsky, negotiated China's entry into the World Trade Organization and, after Clinton left office in 2001, moved to another private Washington law firm, WilmerHale, where she took charge of its China team.

In recent years, the cash and allure of the China business have extended downward from the top levels of the U.S. government to ordinary working-level civil servants. Twenty years ago, a China specialist who left the State Department, CIA, or Pentagon might go off to teach Chinese history or Mandarin at a university. Today, the more common career pattern is to retire from public life and hire on as a private China specialist with a Washington law practice or consulting firm. Leading scholars on China, too, have discovered that they can make money on the side as consultants for companies doing business in China. When the academics write op-ed pieces, testify in Congress, or take part in seminars, they are identified by their jobs at universities; rarely are the additional financial stakes in China business or consulting disclosed. To take one example: In news stories and op-ed articles, China specialist Kenneth Lieberthal is generally described as a leading sinologist, or University of Michigan specialist on China, or former National Security Council aide. All of these descriptions are accurate. Rarely is it mentioned that he has also served as a senior director of Stonebridge International, Berger's consulting firm. (Indeed, in one respect Kissinger is the subject of an odd form of discrimination: When he writes op-ed articles, he is required to disclose that he might have a financial interest in the subject about which he is writing. Most other op-ed writers about China are not subjected to this requirement.)

Many of America's think tanks get sizable donations from business executives and companies that are doing business in China, and the donors seek to foster policies that will protect or augment their financial interests. The think tanks, in turn, issue a flurry of studies and reports supporting trade with China and other policies that favor the American business community. Some of the think tanks go a step further by giving a platform, and thus the appearance of objectivity and impartiality, to major donors with their own private commercial or financial interests in China.

The most flagrant example involved Maurice (Hank) Greenberg, the former chairman and chief executive of American International Group (AIG), one of America's biggest insurers. The company has extensive operations in China; it was the first American insurance firm allowed into the People's Republic after the Chinese revolution. AIG was founded by Cornelius V. Starr, whose first insurance venture, in 1919, was in Shanghai; upon his death, he left his estate to a foundation, the C.V. Starr Foundation. Greenberg served as chairman of the foundation.[8]

Greenberg is a man of intense views, particularly about China. Over the years, he has voiced sympathy for the Chinese leadership and the problems it faces; he has repeatedly belittled the idea that the United States government should give emphasis to human rights or democracy in its policy toward China. "The histories and cultures of countries are vastly different, so it is unrealistic to expect China to have a political system that parallels any other," he wrote recently.[9] These views would hardly be unique, except for the extraordinary role Greenberg has played in propagating them. Through his role as chairman of the C. V. Starr Foundation, he became a leading donor to the Council on Foreign Relations, the Asia Society, the Nixon Center (publisher of *The National Interest*), the Atlantic Council, and several Washington think tanks ranging from the liberal Brookings Institution to the conservative Heritage Foundation. At least a couple of the recipient institutions gave Greenberg a seat on the board: He served as vice chairman of the Council on Foreign Relations, president of the Nixon Center, and chairman of the Asia Society. At times, Greenberg aggressively sought to steer such institutions toward his own views of China policy. In one case, he wrote a letter threatening to cut off Starr's contributions to the Heritage Foundation after one of its China specialists suggested that Congress delay a vote to grant permanent trading rights to China.[10]

This proliferation of donations, consultancies, and retainers for China-related work is not illegal. Business executives like Greenberg may contribute where they please. China specialists have the legal right to earn money, like everyone else; and merely conducting ordinary business in China, or helping and advising others to do it, is not by itself wrong. (It is another story when American companies help China's police and security apparatus in their system of censorship, as some of America's leading Internet and computer companies have done.) The American China experts involved in these ventures by the consulting firms and think tanks usually argue, with sincerity, that they maintain their intellectual independence. They insist that their beliefs about China have not been compromised by their fees or retainers.

This is, however, a remarkable turnabout. For several decades, from the 1940s through at least the 1980s, many of America's leading scholars used to argue with cogency that American policy toward China was being improperly influenced by a web of money, business, and political connections in Washington. This network was originally called the "China lobby" when Chiang Kai-shek's Nationalist regime was in power on the Chinese mainland; later, after the end of the Chinese civil war, it was often referred to as the "Taiwan lobby."[11]

Now, the power of this lobby has been dramatically reduced.[12] There is a much larger, more powerful network of money, scholarship, and business opportunities operating in Washington in support of those who favor policies of "engagement" with the People's Republic of China. Yet somehow, in the midst of this change, the scholars' old, legitimate concerns about the deleterious influence of money on American China policy have been muted.

■ ■ ■

The impact of this deluge of money has been to skew American discussions about China toward an upbeat, pro-business viewpoint. There is a distinctive mind-set that prevails at established institutions in Washington, in the American business community, and in prestige institutions such as the Council on Foreign Relations, the Asia Society, or the Business Roundtable. Not every China specialist thinks alike, of course; nevertheless, one finds a set of recurrent ideas, themes, and attitudes. The underlying tone is one of defensiveness about China's one-party state and an instinctive reluctance, particularly in public, to criticize or even call attention to repression of dissent. In discussions about China, certain subjects and themes are emphasized, while others are downplayed or ignored. Some assumptions are never called into question.

Let's set down as many of these underlying attitudes as possible. Together, they make up what we might call the Credo of the China Elites. It doesn't describe the views of any particular individual; no one believes in the whole list. Rather, it's a composite sketch, a summary of countless conversations over the years with those who call for "engagement" with China's Communist regime and refrain from criticism of it:

1. *China's top leaders (or whoever the prominent Americans have been granted access to on their latest visits to Beijing and Shanghai) are wise but beleaguered.* They have the country's best interests at heart.

2. *In contrast, opponents of the regime should be viewed with skepticism, if not outright hostility.* Those who press for changes in China's one-party system are either self-serving or crazy. Political dissidents in the former Soviet Union or Eastern Europe nearly twenty years ago were worthy of respect; those in China are far less worthy.

3. *There may be rampant corruption in China, but it is the result of unseen low-level officials.* It has nothing to do with the leadership, the Communist Party, or its monopoly on power. Although China's top leaders were generally once lower-level officials themselves, they are all clean; none of the endemic corruption at the lower levels ascended with them to the top.

4. *Repression and censorship in China should not be overemphasized.* Rather, in talking about China, Americans should seize upon any sign, however faint, of future political liberalization. It is less significant that political opponents of the regime are thrown in jail than that China's leaders hint vaguely that they might change the political system at some indefinite point far in the future.

5. *Any tension between America and China is inherently bad and is the responsibility of the United States.* However, if the confrontation involves intellectual property rights or other U.S. commercial interests, then it is China's fault and is a legitimate issue that must be addressed immediately.

6. *Congress is dangerous and should be involved in China policy as little as possible.* Certainly, on other issues such as Iraq, terrorism, intelligence, or the defense budget, presidential power is to be mistrusted, and we are in urgent need of greater legislative oversight. On China, however, the more the executive branch can do without congressional attention, the better.

7. *American public opinion is similarly dangerous.* In general, the less it focuses on China, the better. In particular, public attention should be diverted from arrests, detentions, censorship, or anything else that might raise questions about the nature of China's political system.

8. *What's happening on the ground in China today is whatever Chinese leaders tell visiting Americans is happening.* Everything in China is under control. The turmoil you read about in the newspapers—riots, strikes, and land seizures—is remote and distant and not to be taken too seriously, since it doesn't take place in the central districts of Beijing and Shanghai.

9. *Democracy would be harmful for China.* Or, alternatively: Democracy would be okay for China, and the current leaders like the idea so much that they are planning to introduce it many decades from now—after we (and they) are all dead. Or, as a third alternative: Democracy would be good for China, and even though the leadership is adamantly opposed to democracy, it's going to come to China inevitably anyway.

10. *The Chinese regime now enjoys widespread public support inside China.* Really, it does. The only reason the regime doesn't demonstrate this widespread public support to the rest of the world by holding an election is that . . . it just doesn't.

■   ■   ■

Foreign investment in China brings in huge new sources of money to the emerging elites in China's major cities. It enriches the Chinese consultants who provide advice to Western companies, the Chinese entrepreneurs who start up new businesses, and, often, the Communist Party cadres who approve loans or grant licenses to Chinese business ventures (which, not infrequently, are run by the children or friends of the party cadres). These elites need to keep Chinese wage levels low, so that the foreign investors keep on flooding into China. They have an interest in repressing political dissent so that the country looks quiet and stable to prospective investors. Needless to say, the Chinese business elites strongly support perpetuating the existing state of affairs for as long as possible.

Similarly, American elites are content with the status quo. It enables American firms to shift manufacturing operations to China, where labor costs are low and corporate leaders don't have to worry about independent trade unions.

To be sure, the American and Chinese business elites do not always see eye to eye. American companies sometimes complain that their Chinese partners are ripping off their designs or diverting money from a joint venture. The Chinese executives complain that Americans fail to understand China's culture or the intricate ways in which the Chinese system works. But these are disputes over business operations. In the larger sense, the Chinese and American elites share a common interest in the existing economic order, in which China serves as the world's low-wage, high-volume, all-purpose manufacturing center.

Thus, on the surface it looks as if middle-class Americans are identifying with middle-class Chinese, dreaming that the Chinese, too, will one day insist on a choice of political candidates the way they are now able to select from a range of lattes and mochas at Starbucks. Look beneath the surface, however, and you will find a more troubling reality: The business communities of China and the United States do not harbor these dreams of democracy. Both profit from a Chinese system that permits no political opposition, and—for now, at least—both are content with it.

CHAPTER FOUR

THE P-FACTOR

One day in 1992, a Chinese official fretted over lunch that things seemed not to be going well for his government in the United States. The George H. W. Bush administration was preparing to sell American F-16 warplanes to Taiwan, a landmark change of policy that burst through all prior restrictions on American arms sales to the island. At the same time, the Democratic presidential candidate, Bill Clinton, was excoriating the Republicans for their secretive diplomacy with China; Clinton was proposing that the United States set new human rights conditions on the yearly renewal of China's trade benefits in America. The diplomat asked a question that, at first, I didn't comprehend. "What's happened to the P-factor?" he wondered.

"P-factor?" What was he talking about? Finally, he explained to me. Over the two decades since the Nixon opening to China, the People's Republic of China had discovered that whenever it had difficulties with the lower levels of the U.S. government, it could rely on an American president or his highest aides to intervene with a decision in China's favor.

Disputes in fields like foreign policy and economics are often complicated and multifaceted. The president and his top aides may know far less about the details of a controversy—involving, for example, a region of the world or a particular industry or a health issue—than their subordinates. Nevertheless, these top-level figures may well know how they want the decision to come out and which side they want to win.

This is the P-factor—a White House intervention that will override the working levels of government, sweep aside the complexities, and, in China's case, guide the outcome in favor of the PRC. The P-factor has been evident in American relations with China since the earliest days of the Nixon opening. In late 1971, a few months after Henry Kissinger's initial visit to Beijing, war broke out between India and Pakistan. The U.S. officials who were closely following events on the Indian subcontinent—the State Department and the working-level officials of the National Security Council—believed strongly that the United States should take a detached position toward this war. However, Pakistan was a close friend and ally of China, and it had played the crucial role in arranging Kissinger's historic trip. Grateful to the Pakistanis, Nixon and Kissinger overruled the specialists working beneath them and decreed that the United States would "tilt" toward Pakistan over India—not because of the details of the Indo-Pakistan war, but as an outgrowth of their desire to forge close ties with China.

The P-factor has been at work over and over again in America's relations with China over the past thirty-five years—not only during the 1970s and 1980s, when the United States wanted China's help against the Soviet Union, but also, with brief exceptions, since that time. Although in the current popular imagination Washington is dominated by fire-breathing hawks prejudiced against China, the reality does not fit this caricature. George W. Bush, like all of his predecessors since the Nixon era, has been personally involved in China policy and has taken considerable care to avoid antagonizing the Chinese leadership.

There is nothing wrong with the working of the P-factor. American presidents and their top advisers are entitled to set priorities and to overrule their subordinates. That's what they're supposed to do; it's why we have elections. The difficulties arise when it comes to details. Once a president decides he wants a dispute to come out one way or another, he may have little time to bother with the specifics or the execution. When Jimmy Carter decided he wanted to establish diplomatic ties with the People's Republic of China, for example, he left unclear the nature of America's future relationship to Taiwan (if any)—to the point where Congress had to pass legislation specifying some of the details, and other specifics had to be worked out in subsequent acrimonious negotiations between Washington and Beijing.

Ever since the Nixon opening, Chinese leaders have recognized the importance of establishing personal relationships with American presidents and their top aides. Premier Zhou Enlai's brilliant courtship of Henry Kissinger set the tone. Zhou flattered Kissinger endlessly, and it worked. "No other world leaders have the sweep and imagination of Mao and Chou [sic], nor the capacity and will to pursue a long-range policy," Kissinger wrote to Nixon after one of his long nighttime conversations with the Chinese leaders in Beijing.[1]

There is a pattern to how China works the White House. Typically, Chinese leaders suggest to an American president and his national security adviser that they are wiser and more farsighted than their subordinates or the career bureaucracy or ordinary cabinet members—all of whom, the Chinese suggest, are too bogged down in day-to-day matters and messy details.[2] China represents the wave of the future, so the argument goes; therefore, as a matter of "strategic vision," the top-level Americans ought to steer American policies in favor of the Chinese government. ("Strategy" and "strategic" are common buzzwords in American policy toward China, and the words are often as ill defined and pretentiously futuristic in this context as they are elsewhere. A loose translation might mean "too important for everyday realities." In the corporate world, when an American business executive is suddenly put in charge of "strategic planning," that usually means he or she has been kicked upstairs.)

Let's scrutinize a bit further this hazy notion that "China is the future." Obviously, given the size of China's population and its recent economic growth, China as a nation is likely to take on greater importance in the future. However, China's Communist Party leadership (that is, the Leninist party that now rules China) might well *not* reflect the future—or at least not a future that is in the long-term interests of the people of either China or the United States. Therefore, the U.S. government ought to think twice about doing things that will help to entrench or perpetuate China's current regime. Curiously, American presidents have failed to grasp that if they are indeed trying to be visionary, they should be working to bring about a China that is a democratic country, not a one-party state. The line that "China is the future" does not mean that the United States should today build up, placate, and conciliate its current government.

Yet sadly, every single American president since Nixon has, in one way or another, either ignored or quietly given up on the issue of Chinese democracy. Through their actions, public statements, and rationalizations, the American presidents of the last thirty-five years have all at some point averted their gaze from the Chinese Communist Party's continuing repression of all organized opposition.

RICHARD NIXON

For Nixon, it must be said, the question of democracy in China was never a serious issue. At the time of his opening to Beijing, there was no sign of any democratic movement on the Chinese mainland. The country was still in the midst of the Cultural Revolution (although Mao and Zhou misleadingly told Kissinger that it was over). Across the Taiwan Strait, the government in Taiwan was no more democratic than the People's Republic of China; Chiang

Kai-shek's Nationalist regime may not have been quite as thorough in repressing dissent as Mao Zedong's Communist Party, but it, too, was a one-party regime that tolerated no organized opposition.

Nixon's political skill lay precisely in his ability to sweep aside questions about democracy and repression in China while forming a political consensus in the United States for his China policy. This required a bit of sleight of hand with both liberals and conservatives.

It is often said that Nixon succeeded with conservatives on China because he could draw on his reputation as an anti-Communist. This is true, yet Nixon's political shrewdness also went a few steps further. He had learned during his 1959 "kitchen debate" with Nikita Khrushchev that an American political leader could gain in popularity at home merely by being perceived as "standing up to" the top leaders of the major Communist powers. What counted was to convey a sense of proximity and solemnity. It was not necessary to extract tangible concessions—in fact, the nastier a Communist leader, the more credit the American political leader would derive simply from the meeting itself. These dynamics held true especially for a politician on the Republican Right, who could insinuate that if a liberal Democrat had taken part in the same meeting, he might have given something away. Thus, Nixon, throughout his presidency, pressed for his own political advantage the theme that the Communist leaders he was meeting were nasty people and that he was the only American leader tough enough to deal with them. Political repression didn't really enter into the equation—or if it did, it actually helped Nixon, since under his logic the more brutal the Chinese or Soviet leaders were, the more America needed someone like Nixon.

In dealing with liberals, Nixon felt little need to address the issues of democracy or political repression. Many on the American Left had been arguing for years that the Chinese Communist Party enjoyed greater popular support than had Chiang Kai-shek's Nationalists. Nixon viewed his own opening to China as a matter of hard-nosed balance-of-power diplomacy, and in private he was scornful of liberal attitudes toward China. On one of Nixon's secret tape recordings, he joked with Kissinger and his political aide Chuck Colson about how they had deluded liberals into believing Nixon thought the way they did. Yet in public he was willing to court the Left by emphasizing the romance of the new American relationship with China.

Nixon's China initiative became an important component of his 1972 reelection campaign; it enabled him to win the support of moderate and independent voters by demonstrating that he was willing to change and to challenge traditional Republican orthodoxy. Throughout Nixon's presidency and that of his post-Watergate successor, Gerald Ford, amid the euphoria of the opening to China, virtually no one was eager to linger too long on the subject of democracy or human rights. Today, many Chinese look back upon the Cultural Revolution as lasting a full decade, from 1966 until after Mao's death in 1976; but in Washington during the Nixon and Ford years, few spoke of the Cultural Revolution as an ongoing affair. The subject was rarely discussed.

All of their successors in the White House, however, have been obliged to deal with the questions arising from China's continuing severe repression of political dissent. Talking about China confronted each president with a conundrum: how to square his general foreign policy or philosophy or reputation with the unpleasant realities of China's Leninist system. The unfolding series of evasions and rationalizations about China were passed on from one White House to another. Taken collectively, they make up the core of American thinking on China today.

JIMMY CARTER

For Carter, Chinese repression was an awkward subject because of his administration's oft stated commitment to human rights. In the wake of the Vietnam War, Carter had sought some new, principled basis for American foreign policy that would replace, or go beyond, the anti-Communism of the 1950s and 1960s, and human rights became the touchstone. Recasting American policy as a struggle for human rights enabled Carter to continue to oppose political repression in the Soviet Union and Eastern Europe, as the United States had in the past. But Carter's new policy also meant that human rights principles would be applied to authoritarian leaders allied with the United States, such as the shah of Iran and Anastasio Somoza Debayle of Nicaragua.

The unanswered question was whether or how Carter's human rights policy would extend to China. The subject arose in 1978–1979, with the Democracy Wall movement in Beijing. For a brief time, Chinese authorities permitted ordinary citizens to put up wall posters expressing their views; the leader of the movement, Wei Jingsheng, took the extraordinary step of calling openly for democracy. When Carter gave a speech in Washington on worldwide human rights, a wall poster went up the next day in Beijing that read, "We would like to ask you to pay attention to the state of human rights in China."[3] Within a few months after the beginning of the Democracy Wall campaign, however, Deng Xiaoping consolidated his control over the Communist Party; the wall posters came down, and leaders of the movement, including Wei Jingsheng, were jailed.

What to do? The Carter administration came up with a rationalization for looking the other way, one that has endured in one form or another ever since: Yes, China was repressing political dissent, but at least the situation in China was vastly better than it had been during the Cultural Revolution. The standard for judging Chinese repression, in other words, was not any of its contemporaneous conduct, but how these actions compared with the rock-bottom misery of the Cultural Revolution. This line of argument, which we might call the "Cultural Revolution baseline," persists in intellectual discussions of China even to the present day. The Cultural Revolution baseline can be used to excuse virtually any sort of repression in China, since none of it can match the horrors of the Cultural Revolution. (Applying this same logic, of course, we might say that the East German security apparatus was an improvement over the Nazis.) The question that is rarely asked is why we should judge the Chinese regime today by the standards of Cultural Revolution, rather than by comparison with other Asian governments today, such as those of Taiwan, South Korea, Japan, the Philippines, India, and Indonesia, all of which are more willing than China to permit dissent and organized political opposition.

RONALD REAGAN

Ronald Reagan felt no compulsion to justify his China policy on human rights grounds. He had come to office committed to reversing the changes of the Carter administration, including the emphasis on human rights. Reagan made clear during his 1980 campaign that he would restore the legitimacy of anti-Communism as the bedrock of American foreign policy. In his early years of office, he pushed through massive increases in defense spending and denounced the Soviet Union as "the evil empire." Yet Reagan's anti-Communism, like Carter's human rights policy, raised the question "What about China?" At the end of a trip to the Chinese mainland in 1984, Reagan offered his own memorable evasion. Talking to reporters, he referred to the PRC as "this so-called Communist China." This was a shrewd formulation, one that deflected attention from the unchanged nature of China's political system and enabled Reagan to keep on denouncing political repression in the Soviet Union, while saying virtually nothing about similar conduct in China.

China's economic system was, in fact, just beginning to open up, in ways that would increasingly depart from Communist orthodoxy. Yet China was still run along traditional Leninist lines by a Communist Party that permitted no organized opposition. By using the phrase *so-called Communist*, Reagan was conflating economics and politics and was suggesting inaccurately that because China's economic system was in the process of liberalization, its political system was changing, too. This confusion, too, became permanently enshrined in American perceptions of China: Starting in the 1980s, whenever critics asked about repression of dissent, defenders would often reply that China was changing, even though, in political terms, it usually was not.

Overall, Reagan chose to concentrate during his eight years in office on the Soviet Union, not China. Like his three predecessors, Reagan came to view China primarily as a partner against the Soviet Union, and his rhetoric and actions reflected this underlying reality. On a trip to Moscow in 1988, Reagan met face-to-face with ninety-six Soviet dissidents at the residence of the American ambassador. He never did anything comparable with respect to China. In 1988, when Reagan's ambassador to China, Winston Lord, met with Chinese students in a seminar at Beijing University (a considerably more modest step than Reagan's personal warmth toward Soviet dissidents), Deng Xiaoping sent a personal, angry warning to Washington, and the Reagan administration quickly backed off. Since Nixon's day, American leaders had dealt with China only through its Communist Party leadership and had avoided identification with dissidents or opponents of the regime. Reagan showed no interest in disturbing this status quo.[4]

GEORGE H. W. BUSH

George H. W. Bush took office intending to steer American foreign policy back to the nonjudgmental realism of Nixon and Henry Kissinger. From the outset, Bush the elder avoided emphasizing either human rights, as Carter had, or anti-Communism, in the fashion of Reagan. Bush's national security adviser, Brent Scowcroft, had been Kissinger's deputy, and Bush himself had served during the Ford administration as head of the U.S. mission in Beijing while Kissinger was secretary of state. Yet in dealing with China, Bush was soon confronted with realities that Nixon and Kissinger had never faced. In June 1989, less than a half year after Bush was sworn in, Deng Xiaoping sent the People's Liberation Army into downtown Beijing to eradicate the massive, continuing demonstrations at Tiananmen Square, killing hundreds or perhaps thousands of people in the process. Similar protests in other Chinese cities were also brought to a halt, and the Chinese Communist Party followed up with a series of arrests and show trials.

Meanwhile, Eastern Europe was opening up. Poland elected its first non-Communist government in June 1989, on the same day as the Tiananmen massacre; and over the following months, there were further steps toward liberalization in Hungary and Czechoslovakia. This movement culminated in November 1989 when crowds of East Germans tore down the Berlin Wall. The cold war between America and the Soviet Union was coming to a close.

Thus, in a period of six months in 1989, the two linchpins that had held up American policy toward China since the early 1970s were suddenly cut away: first, the notion that the Chinese political system was gradually opening up; and second, the belief that America needed cooperation from China to counteract the military threat from the Soviet Union. What should the United States say or do, then, about the nature of China's political system, which by this time was plain for all to see? There were two elements to Bush's response. First, the president and his administration rushed to perpetuate, in a new era, the notion that China's geopolitical importance should outweigh American concerns about political repression in the PRC. The perceptions of China's overriding significance had, of course, been based on the Soviet threat to the United States, and now this threat was disappearing. Did that mean America would now condemn China's Leninist regime in the same fashion as the Soviet Union or the Communist governments of Eastern Europe? The Bush administration's answer was no: Despite the end of the cold war, China remained of great strategic importance to the United States. The president groped to explain exactly why. In one press conference, he suggested that the

United States now needed China as a restraint on rising Japanese power; but since Japan was an American ally, the president quickly dropped this line of argument. Bush administration officials next began to argue that China was important to the United States because it could do nasty things, such as export missiles. By the end of the Bush administration, after the American military triumph in the Gulf War, it began to appear as if Bush and his top aides were themselves quietly beginning to downgrade China's significance to U.S. policy. It was during this period that Bush opened the way for the sale of American jet fighters to Taiwan and Chinese officials began to worry about losing the P-factor.

The second element in Bush's response to the upheavals of 1989 was the policy of "engagement." Although Bush had announced in public a freeze on high-level contacts between American and Chinese officials, he secretly sent Scowcroft to Beijing for talks with Deng Xiaoping in July 1989 and again five months later. After the visits were criticized, Bush explained that he didn't want to isolate China. He wanted, instead, a "comprehensive policy of engagement" with China.[5] The choice of words was surprising, because the Reagan administration had only a few years earlier used the term *constructive engagement* to describe its policy of dealing with South Africa's apartheid government.

"Engagement" became the principal catchword used to describe and justify American policy toward China's one-party state, and it has endured to the present day. The suggestion was that sheer contact would serve to moderate or alter China's political system. Yet the policy of engagement is simply a process, one that merely prescribes continued contacts; if China's repression becomes more severe, then under the logic of engagement, the solution is to have more meetings. Engagement says nothing about results. It does not require any changes in policy on the part of the "engagee." The implication is that the "engager" will not let the behavior of the Chinese regime, however reprehensible, get in the way of continued business with China.

And continued business was, indeed, the purpose. Under the George H. W. Bush administration, the policy of engagement became the justification for a gradual return to business as usual. In economic terms, this was a crucial period in China. In those days, China was nothing like the economic powerhouse it became in the mid-1990s. Indeed, although this period is little remembered now, the Chinese economy was quite fragile in the two years after the Tiananmen crackdown. The Japanese government had suspended a package of $5.6 billion in loans to China after the massacre, and the World Bank froze more than $2 billion in new interest-free loans. Economic growth dropped to such low levels that, for a time, there was fear of a recession.

If ever there was a time when the United States held considerable economic leverage over China, this was it. The Bush administration didn't seek to use this leverage. Under his policy of engagement, the senior Bush opened the way for a resumption of World Bank and Japanese loans to China and gradually restored normal contacts. Within a couple of years, Deng Xiaoping succeeded spectacularly in reviving China's economic growth, and by the time Bush gave way to a new administration in Washington, the moment of American economic leverage had passed.

BILL CLINTON

The central figure in developing America's post–cold war approach to Chinese repression was Bill Clinton. The elder Bush had been a transitional figure, seeking to preserve the status quo and the old Nixon-era relationship with China amid dramatic changes elsewhere in the world. It was during Clinton's presidency that the principal post–cold war battles over China policy were waged. Clinton eventually came up with the enduring justification for American inaction in the face of China's continuing eradication of dissent. It was the Clinton administration that managed to turn black into white and white into black—to persuade Americans that it was somehow politically progressive and intellectually sophisticated to accept Chinese repression and uncouth or unenlightened to attempt to combat it.

During the George H. W. Bush administration, the Democratic Congress had twice approved bills that would have tied the renewal of China's annual trade benefits to specific, tangible improvements in human rights. The proposed legislation, sponsored by Senate majority leader George Mitchell and Representative Nancy Pelosi, attracted considerable Republican support. On both occasions, Bush vetoed the legislation. As a presidential candidate, Clinton endorsed these bills, denounced the Bush administration, and, in accepting the Democratic nomination, pledged "an America that will not coddle dictators, from Baghdad to Beijing."

Once in the White House, Clinton proceeded to put into effect the policy of the congressional Democrats. He did so, however, with one modification: Instead of seeking passage of the Mitchell-Pelosi legislation, he persuaded Democratic leaders to accept a presidential executive order that would adopt the same approach, linking trade and human rights. That change proved to be of decisive importance, because it is always easier to abandon an executive order than a congressional statute. Clinton's executive order took effect in May 1993 and would have limited China's trade benefits a year later if there were not sufficient progress on human rights in the meantime. During that year, American business executives grew increasingly anxious about the prospect of losing trade with China; the Chinese economy had by this time begun its new phase of startlingly rapid growth. Clinton's own economic advisers and some of his campaign contributors began crusading against his human rights policy. In May 1994, just as the deadline approached, Clinton retreated. While admitting the human rights climate in China hadn't improved significantly, Clinton declined to impose the penalties he had promised a year earlier. Instead he revoked his own executive order, abandoning his party's approach of the previous four years.

Clinton's reversal was, in many ways, a watershed. His decision set American policy toward China onto a new course for the post–cold war era. It reflected the reality that commerce had become the dominant factor in America's view of China and also illustrated China's growing ability to use the lure of its market as leverage in dealing with Washington. In a larger sense, these events of 1993–1994 also helped determine the future direction of the Clinton administration, the Democratic Party, and American political thought. The turnabout on China—combined with Clinton's support for the North American Free Trade Agreement—solidified a close and enduring link between Clinton's Democratic Party and the business community. It also helped foster the growing speculation in the mid-1990s that the world had entered into a new age of globalization. Clinton, meanwhile, was redefining what it meant to be a liberal; in Clinton's version, liberalism was intrinsically linked to the core value of promoting free trade, much as it had been in nineteenth-century Britain.

In the early stages of his presidential campaign, Clinton had questioned whether China was so important to the United States in the post–cold war world. Referring to the Nixon-era metaphor that America was playing a "China card" against the Soviet Union, Clinton had observed that it made no sense to play the China card when there was no longer anyone else (that is, the Soviet Union) at the table. In other words, he was suggesting that China's geopolitical significance to the United States had diminished because of the end of the cold war. Two years later, in his decision to abandon the linkage between trade and human rights, Clinton made plain that in a new era, China was once again profoundly important to the United States, not for its cooperation against the Soviet Union, but above all as an outlet for American commerce and investment.

Clinton's 1994 trade decision reopened the question "What should be done about Chinese repression?" The president had decided that the attempt to restrict trade with China was not politically acceptable—but then what? Should the United States try some other approach? Or should it simply accept China's one-party state as a permanent fixture of international life? Neither the American public nor the Clinton administration was willing to admit to a policy of sheer acceptance.

Clinton's answer came in two phases. First, in 1994, as he was abandoning the policy of trade linkage, Clinton announced a "new human rights strategy"—a package of measures aimed at helping to ease political repression in China without restricting trade opportunities. American businesses would be encouraged to adopt codes of conduct for their operations in China. Radio programming to China would be increased. The United States would seek to win passage for a condemnation of China at the United Nations Human Rights Commission.

It seemed questionable from the start that any of these measures would bring about much change in China. Within three years, Clinton administration officials were beginning to acknowledge that there had not been much progress. Nevertheless, at the beginning of his second term, Clinton was eager to take new steps with the Chinese regime.

So in 1997, Clinton came up with a different answer to the problem of Chinese repression. Under this new formulation, the United States did not really need to do anything concrete, except continue to trade with China. The increased foreign trade with China and investment in China would eventually lead to an opening of China's political system, whether the Chinese Communist Party wanted these changes or not.

This was the "inevitability" argument—or, to put it another way, the Soothing Scenario. The president contended that democracy and liberty were inexorably going to come to China anyway, just as they had come to Eastern Europe, leading to the fall of the Berlin Wall. China was on the "wrong side of history," Clinton declared. Its one-party state could do nothing to prevent its own eventual demise. At the end of a 1998 visit to China, the first by an American president since the Tiananmen massacre, Clinton predicted democratic change was coming to the world's most populous nation. Asked whether there could ever be democracy in China, he replied, "I believe there can be and there will be."[6]

In his final year in office, Clinton succeeded in winning approval for the most far-reaching of all his initiatives on China. Congress enacted legislation opening the way for China to become a member of the World Trade Organization, thus ending the need for China to obtain annual renewals of its trade privileges. No longer could Congress threaten to curb China's trade benefits; they were now permanent. The legislation followed several years of effort by the Clinton administration, both in negotiating with China and in preparing the American public for the change.

In urging China's entry into the WTO, some Clinton administration officials argued that the change would help reduce America's trade imbalance with China. "[China's membership] would give the United States more access to China's market, boost our exports, *reduce our trade deficit*, and create new, well-paying jobs," asserted Secretary of State Madeleine Albright. (Emphasis added.)[7] For his part, Clinton campaigned for China's WTO membership by suggesting repeatedly that it would help bring political freedom to China. "It is likely to have a profound impact on human rights and political liberty," he predicted.[8]

Albright's forecast about cutting the trade deficit was clearly wrong. The American trade imbalance with China was about $15 billion a year when Clinton took office, about $70 billion a year in 2000 at the time Congress approved its entry into the WTO, and about $200 billion a year at the end of 2005. Clinton's predictions about democracy and political freedom coming to China have not been borne out, either.

GEORGE W. BUSH

With the arrival of George W. Bush, the P-factor took on a more personal dimension. The Chinese leadership had forged long-standing ties to the Bush family, dating back to the 1970s, when Bush's father had served as head of the U.S. liaison office in Beijing. Bush's uncle Prescott Bush Jr. had extensive business ties in China. To underscore this personal relationship, the Chinese government immediately sent as its new ambassador to the United States a polished diplomat, Yang Jiechi, who had been a friend of the Bush family since 1977, when he had served as host and interpreter for the elder Bush on an extensive tour of China and Tibet. To the Bush clan, the new ambassador was known as "Tiger" Yang.

When the younger Bush arrived in the White House in 2001, there was considerable speculation that his administration would be more confrontational in dealing with China. Bush himself had termed China a "strategic competitor" during his campaign, and his new administration included several leading neoconservatives in its middle and upper ranks.

In fact, however, Bush steered American China policy along the same path as had his predecessors. Bush himself never used the phrase "strategic competitor" after he was sworn in. Within months, he angered neoconservatives by sending a carefully worded apology to Beijing to end a weeklong dispute over the collision of a Chinese jetfighter with an American reconnaissance plane. After the September 11 attacks, and particularly in 2002, when Bush was preparing to go to war in Iraq and needed China's support (or acquiescence) at the UN Security Council, it was clear that the George W. Bush administration was eager for a quiet, stable working relationship with the Chinese regime. To be sure, there were some within the Bush administration, particularly in Secretary of Defense Donald Rumsfeld's Pentagon, who warned about the growing power of the People's Liberation Army and wanted America's China policy to take on a harder, more hawkish edge. But the president wouldn't go along. He became personally involved in China policy, and when he intervened he generally sought to avoid tensions with the leadership in Beijing. The contrast was striking: On Iraq and the larger Middle East, Bush settled disputes within his administration by siding with the hawks; on China, however, the president weighed in on the side of the doves.

But then, what about democracy in China? For George W. Bush, that question seemed even more awkward than it had been for other presidents, because of Bush's frequent and insistent rhetoric about democracy elsewhere in the world. In speech after speech, he spoke of democracy as the linchpin of his foreign policy. "It is the policy of the United States to seek and support the growth of democratic movements and institutions in every nation and culture, with the ultimate goal of ending tyranny in our world," Bush said in his second inaugural address. ". . . Democratic reformers facing repression, prison or exile can know: America sees you for who you are: The future leaders of a free country."[9] Bush's usual response was just to ignore the problem. Sometimes in his speeches, he gave a quick rundown of the world's leading undemocratic regimes; invariably, China was left off the list. Consider, for example, his 2006 State of the Union speech. "At the start of 2006, more than half the people of our world live in democratic nations," Bush said. "And we do not forget the other half—in places like Syria and Burma, Zimbabwe, North Korea and Iran—because the demands of justice, and the peace of this world, require their freedom as well."[10]

This careful two-sentence formulation bears a bit more scrutiny. Where did China fit in? Certainly not in Bush's first sentence; the Chinese people do not live in a democratic nation. So was China, then, in "the other half—*in places like Syria and Burma, Zimbabwe, North Korea and Iran*"? Bush didn't want to mention China by name in such bad company. So perhaps China was hidden behind those seemingly bland words *places like*. . . . Those five undemocratic countries named by Bush have a combined population of about 166 million people—roughly one-eighth the size of undemocratic China. Iran, for all its many political failings, did in fact have elections. It was hard to escape the conclusion either that Bush had some special, unarticulated definition of the word *democracy* that was different from its ordinary meaning or that when he talked about democracy, he forgot about China.

Bush's approach to Chinese democracy was on display when he visited China in the fall of 2005. At the time, the Chinese regime headed by President Hu Jintao was in the midst of an intensified drive against political dissent. Journalists were being jailed, newspapers were being censored, and lawyers who represented opponents of the regime were being harassed. On the eve of Bush's visit, Chinese security officials detained a number of dissidents or put them under house arrest.

Bush's response was to adhere closely to the Soothing Scenario. He repeatedly suggested that as China's economy developed and the country grew more prosperous, democracy and freedom would come to China, too. He raised the familiar but dubious comparison with South Korea and Taiwan. "I think about South Korea," Bush told reporters in Beijing. "South Korea opened its economy up and then political reforms followed." In fact, Bush maintained, China's leaders could do nothing to stop the inexorable change.[11]

So as Bush phrased it, there was nothing American leaders needed to do for democracy in China, since democracy was coming anyway, carried in by impersonal historical forces. Under this way of thinking, it would be nice if Chinese Communist Party leaders took steps to end repression and their one-party state—but if they didn't, there was no reason for worry and no grounds for condemnation, because it didn't matter, ultimately, what the Chinese leaders did. Democracy and freedom were on the way.

All of these claims were questionable. China isn't South Korea. The Chinese people have discovered over the past half century that doors opened a crack can be suddenly slammed shut. And it remains unclear that economic advancement leads inevitably to political liberalization. Nevertheless, Bush embraced these ideas, as

Clinton had before him; on China, there was little to distinguish the Republican president from his Democratic predecessor. Democracy was a cause Bush invoked around the world, but one he pursued in some places, not others. Like Carter's human rights policy or Reagan's anti-Communism, Bush's campaign for democracy didn't include China.

CHAPTER FIVE

LET THE
GAMES BEGIN

Get ready. Over the coming months, before and during the Beijing Olympics of 2008, you will be bombarded with the stereotypes about China that have accumulated over hundreds of years. This will not be just an ordinary summer Olympics, another quadrennial occasion like the ones in, say, Athens or Sydney or Atlanta. Rather, this time the Olympics will be widely viewed as an epochal event, symbolizing the emergence of China as a world power. The coverage will be on a scale that dwarfs all the previous games.

So the newsmagazines and newspaper headlines about the Olympics will dredge up, over and over again, the same clichéd phrases that have been applied to China so many times before. They will use or make puns on the handful of phrases about China that come from movie titles, famous events, or historical quotes: *The China Syndrome. The Last Emperor. The Long March. The Great Wall. The Cultural Revolution. The Great Leap Forward. The Sleeping Giant Wakes. Crouching Tiger, Hidden Dragon. Marco Polo. The Boxer Rebellion.* Radio and television will accompany their reports with the stock background sounds of traditional

Chinese music: the gentle strings of the pipa, the harsh clang of cymbals.

And television programs about the Olympics will display, hour after hour, the same visual images, which have already been used over and over again. Here's a brief list of television's standard China graphics. See which viewer can check them all off first during coverage of the summer games in 2008.

Traditional symbols of China: Dragons. Lions. The Great Wall. Chinese calligraphy. The Chinese national flag. Pandas. Jade. Xian's Terra Cotta warriors. The shrouded, misty mountains of Guilin. Chopsticks. Bamboo. The Gate of Heavenly Peace. The Temple of Heaven. Tang, Qing, and Ming dynasty porcelain. Shaolin temple and martial arts.

Symbols of a bygone China: Peasants carrying heavy burdens on shoulder poles. Aristocrats in pigtails. Women in *qipao* dresses. Women with bound feet. Masses of city dwellers on bikes. Elderly men with birdcages. Happy peasants. Outdoor exercise classes.

Symbols of modernized China: Young Chinese in discos. Traffic jams. Young Chinese in business suits. Shanghai's television tower. Young Chinese in front of computers. The stock market. Young Chinese in jeans talking on cell phones. Shanghai neon at night.

Symbols of political China: Mao Zedong. Mao swimming in the Yangtze River. Mao and Nixon. Chinese crowds parading victims during the Cultural Revolution. The Goddess of Liberty at Tiananmen Square. The man in front of the tank.

Very few of these televised images or clichés will tell us anything new about China. Instead, they will serve mostly to reinforce what we already know or think we know. At worst, some of the crudest and most ignorant of America's clichés about China refer to things that have never existed in China itself: Take, for example, the American jokes of the 1950s generation about choosing from "column A" and "column B," a crude cliché that originated with the English-language menus in Chinese restaurants in the United States. Television coverage of the Olympics in China generally won't stoop this low (except maybe once or twice).

■ ■ ■

Yet many of these media clichés serve another function besides mere reinforcement of the familiar. They exoticize China, making it seem strange, distant, and difficult to comprehend. The subtext of these portrayals seems to be that China is fundamentally different from the rest of the world, that a visitor to China should suspend his or her ordinary judgments, that the reactions that would be evoked elsewhere in the world have no place in China. (And from these dubious propositions, it is only a short step to the myth that ordinary Chinese don't care about having a say in how their government is run, even though people want such things elsewhere in the world.)

Another subtext of the television coverage is that modern-day China is cute. Ever since China began to emerge from the Cultural Revolution, the rest of the world has treated the country's progress with an air of patronizing bemusement. A correspondent serving in China once said in exasperation that his job was to find "aren't they crazy?" stories about the strange things Chinese people do, so that at the very end of an American network news broadcast, an anchorman could turn up the corners of his mouth into a hint of a smile and say, *"And in China . . . "*—as though China were somehow detached from the rest of the world and of interest mostly for entertainment. The message of these portrayals seems to be that China is not to be taken seriously, that its repressive political system is of no great consequence.

In the years leading up to the Beijing Olympics, China seemed to be actively cultivating a cute-and-cuddly image. In November 2005, it adopted official mascots for the games known as the Five Friendlies—saccharine cartoon drawings of five doll-like characters, including the inevitable panda, all designed to appeal to children, marketers, and tourist shops throughout the world.

In short, this foreign media coverage of the 2008 Beijing Olympics will, in all likelihood, be unconsciously tailored to fit the Soothing Scenario for China's future. In the Olympics programs broadcast in the United States, Europe, and elsewhere, chances are that image after image, set piece after set piece, profile after profile, will convey the theme that China is moving in the right direction. The TV coverage will likely suggest that all problems are manageable, that any step backward will be followed by two steps forward—and that eventually trade and prosperity will bring freedom and democracy to China.

Should we really expect otherwise? The Olympics are big business. Every four years, America's leading companies and, more generally, the world's leading multinational corporations play an ever larger role in putting on the games and, above all, in sponsoring the television coverage of the games. This has been true in all the Olympic cities. Now, for the first time, the Olympics will be in China, where these same multinational corporations have been falling over one another to establish a foothold. The Chinese regime has a long record of being willing to punish those corporations that are judged to be "unfriendly." Will the world's leading car manufacturers and beer companies want to sponsor television coverage of the Olympics that dwells on the unpleasant side of China—the sweatshops, the poverty, the political prisoners, the corruption, the environmental disasters? Not likely.

Of course, most of the television coverage of the Olympics will be just about sports. But when the broadcasting networks fill out their Olympic programs with feature stories about life in China, it's a safe bet that this coverage will bring forth the old clichés and the Soothing Scenario.

■ ■ ■

What sort of Olympics will these be, and what sorts of values will the Chinese regime put forward? Will the Beijing Olympics prove to be comparable to earlier games in, say, Rome in 1960 or Tokyo in 1964 or Seoul in 1988—serving as showcases for nations that had recovered from the devastations of the past and had succeeded in opening up their political systems? Or will the Beijing Olympics follow the much darker precedent of the Berlin Olympics of 1936, an ominous demonstration not merely of national recovery, but of an ugly new era of assertiveness and intolerance?

Amid the blizzard of outside television coverage of the 2008 Beijing Olympics, China will be covering itself on television, too. Chinese television will have its own clichés, but they will be different ones. In many ways, this separate domestic Olympic coverage on China's television stations, carefully controlled by the Chinese regime, will be of greater significance than the foreign coverage. The images that the Chinese regime presents to the Chinese people on domestic TV during the Olympics will tell us a good deal about where the leadership hopes to take the country in the future.

Will the emphasis be on openness, diversity, and tolerance of different points of view, including political points of view? Or will the main themes be sheer national unity and power? The arrival of the Olympics will undoubtedly provide the occasion for an outpouring of Chinese patriotism, as indeed the Olympics have for many other countries in the past. The question is how China's Communist leadership will define patriotism.

The precedents on Chinese TV are not encouraging. During the late 1990s, China celebrated two historical milestones, both with elaborate television extravaganzas. The first, on July 1, 1997, was the return of Hong Kong from Britain to China; the second, on October 1, 1999, was the fiftieth anniversary of the founding of the People's Republic of China. Both times the Chinese regime, then headed by Jiang Zemin, orchestrated massive displays of nationalist sentiment aimed at showing that the Chinese people were unified in support of their government.

The fiftieth-anniversary celebrations of 1999 were particularly egregious. The television coverage featured a parade designed to demonstrate Chinese military power and the achievements of the Communist Party. John Pomfret of *The Washington Post*, one of the most experienced foreign correspondents in Beijing, described the parade that day:

> *No random spectators were allowed to view the scores of gaily colored floats that coursed for two hours down to the Boulevard of Eternal Peace. No overweight children were among the goose-stepping young students. Women participants were picked for their beauty; soldiers were carefully selected for height, polish and marching skill. And all were chosen on the basis of their "love of the motherland," Chinese officials said.*[1]

Perhaps the Beijing Olympics will be different. After all, it can be argued that the 1999 events, by definition, had to concentrate on the rule of the Communist Party (this was, after all, what the fiftieth anniversary was honoring, because no other political group has been allowed to hold any power in China since 1949). By contrast, the Olympics are intended merely to honor sports and, more broadly, the recognition of Beijing as an international city. Still, it is possible that the Chinese leadership will seize upon the occasion of the Olympics to present a domestic political message. The regime may again engage in self-glorification and seek to convey the message that the Chinese Communist Party is the embodiment of and the sole legitimate vehicle for Chinese patriotism. Authorities may well keep away from Chinese television any images of discord.

Will Chinese television convey any sense of political pluralism? Will it be willing to show that not all of the country's 1.3 billion people think alike, that there are honest disagreements among various groups and interests inside the country? Or will the Olympics be the vehicle for further propaganda portraying the myth of national unity? If there are political demonstrations inside China before or during the Olympics, will Chinese television be willing to show them?

If the answer to these questions is no, if the regime instead uses the Olympics to portray to its domestic audience a China that is increasingly powerful but also politically monolithic, then that coverage will be an early portent of the Third Scenario. Such television coverage would serve as a preview of a Chinese future in which increasing wealth does not bring democracy, a China in which rapidly growing economic and military power can be accompanied by continuing political repression.

■ ■ ■

What about the Upheaval Scenario for China's future, the prospect that the country might fall apart? How might that be reflected in Beijing in 2008?

The possibility of demonstrations at the Olympics presents, for China's leaders, a nightmare. China's leaders all remember the sequence of events in the spring of 1989, the tumultuous demonstrations in Tiananmen Square and the prolonged debate within the Communist Party leadership over how to respond. One of the main contributing factors was the visit to Beijing by Soviet leader Mikhail Gorbachev.

Gorbachev's trip was meant to be a watershed, the first summit meeting between the two countries in three decades. The China leadership had made elaborate plans for the visit. And China was not alone. News organizations throughout the United States, Europe, and Japan all sent large teams of reporters and camera crews to cover the events. On the one hand, the presence of Gorbachev and the television cameras helped to stimulate the demonstrations in Tiananmen Square. On the other hand, it also inhibited the Chinese leadership from cracking down.

The Beijing Olympics of 2008 could present many of the same dynamics and the same difficulties. Once again, the presence of a huge international press corps could help to spur on political demonstrations. People or groups seeking to protest the policies of the Chinese government—democracy activists, religious groups, Falun Gong, Tibetans, Uighurs, aggrieved workers and peasants— will have an unparalleled opportunity to attract worldwide attention to their grievances, if they can somehow break through the security meant to keep them away from the television cameras. Meanwhile, Chinese authorities may well be reluctant to use force against such protests during the Olympics.

The result will almost certainly be a massive effort by China's internal security apparatus to head off demonstrations before they start. Would-be protesters will be kept out of Beijing (or if they live in the city, they may be thrown out of Beijing). Crowds will not be allowed to gather; if they do, they will be dispersed before they can move to any public space. The police will be especially rough on groups seeking access to Tiananmen Square, which has been off-limits to protests since 1989.

■　■　■

The Olympics will amount to a test, the greatest one ever, of how China handles short-term visitors to the country. Chinese leaders have long been adept at entertaining guests from overseas and persuading them that everything is under control. Sometimes Chinese officials even manage to charm visitors from democratic countries into yearning for an authoritarian political system that looks better from a distance than it does to those who have to live with its day-to-day realities.

On one visit to China, *New York Times* columnist Thomas L. Friedman confessed he was envious of the Chinese system, "where leaders can, and do, just order that problems be solved." He continued:

> *For instance, Shanghai's deputy mayor told me that as his city became more polluted, the government simply moved thousands of small manufacturers out of Shanghai to clean up the air. . . . At this time, when democracies, like India and America, seem incapable of making hard decisions, I cannot help but feel a tinge of jealousy at China's ability to be serious about its problems and actually do things that are tough and require taking things away from people.[2]*

Friedman's column seemed to accept the deputy mayor's account at face value. He did not report the perspective of the small manufacturers in question, some of whom would probably have complained to him about corruption (did some companies use money or official connections to circumvent the policy?). Nor did Friedman address the bottom-line question of whether the policy worked. Shanghai's air remains hazy, and in general, satellite photos have shown that Chinese cities have some of the worst air pollution in the world.[3]

Chinese leaders are skillful at conveying the impression that the country is already moving in whatever direction arriving visitors want them to go. This phenomenon did not start with China's Communist regime. It has deep roots in Chinese history and has its origins in China's effort to fend off pressure for change from the outside world. During World War II, Chiang Kai-shek's Nationalist regime used to deflect complaints by President Roosevelt about corruption or about Chiang's less than vigorous military campaign against Japan by taking in high-level emissaries from the United States and showing them what great progress Chiang was making.

The current regime is at least as skillful in handling visitors as were Chiang's Nationalists and other predecessors. If, for example, an American delegation is coming to China to complain about copyright violations, the regime may announce a few days in advance that it is planning to crack down on copyright violators. Or the U.S. delegation may arrive in Beijing on a Sunday night and wake up Monday to find a story in the *China Daily*, the state-controlled English-language newspaper, "reporting" that China plans to revise its copyright legislation. Oh, says the visitor, China is already on the right track.

In May 1998, then secretary of state Madeleine Albright landed in China to lay the groundwork for a visit by President Clinton. She had planned to give a speech in Beijing on the subject of the rule of law. Shortly after she arrived, the *China Daily* "coincidentally" published a story about what China was planning to do to improve the rule of law. When the time came for her speech, Albright proudly held up that day's newspaper to her audience as a sign the situation in China was already getting better. "Clearly, both your leaders and your citizens recognize the need to strengthen the rule of law," she said. She did not seem to grasp that the newspaper story was not some random, independent bit of journalism but had been timed specifically to influence her and her trip.

In that same spring of 1998, while Clinton was deciding whether to visit China, the Chinese leadership suggested on a number of occasions that change was in the air. There was talk of political reform, of a new "Beijing spring," of a loosening of controls on political debate. In the end, Clinton decided to make the trip. On the day he arrived in China, a handful of dissidents moved to establish an opposition party, the China Democratic Party. That event, too, was taken as a sign of change in China. That fall, as the top representative of the United Nations Human Rights Commission was preparing her own trip to China, the authorities said they might consider letting the China Democratic Party operate in some provinces.

Clinton and the UN representative had smooth visits to China. Then, at the end of 1998, after all these prominent visitors had returned home, Chinese authorities made their move. They cracked down on the fledgling party, ended its operations, and sent all its leaders to jail. The talk of a Beijing spring ended, as it often does, with the reality of Beijing winter.

We can expect these same dynamics in 2008, but on a far grander scale. Before the summer Olympics, as visitors are preparing to come to Beijing, Chinese leaders will undoubtedly tell the world that change is coming, that their political system is opening up. They will, in fact, probably take some tantalizing actions, ones that hold out the prospect of far-reaching change. In the spring of 2008, China's newspapers and other news media may, for a time, be permitted unprecedented freedom. At Chinese universities and think tanks, intellectuals will launch new explorations of the concept of checks and restraints on the power of the ruling Chinese Communist Party—for example, by increasing the power of the National People's Congress, China's toothless legislature. In general, as the Olympics approach, there will probably be a period of greater tolerance for dissent and for political opposition.

This is the China that will be on display for the tens of thousands of visitors who come to Beijing for the Olympics. China's leaders will want the visitors to see a country that is enlightened, open-minded, and on the verge of far-reaching political change. The first test for the regime, as mentioned previously, will be whether it can protect its image during the games by keeping its citizenry under control. If things work out right, the foreign guests will never see or know how hard China's Ministry of State Security is working to prevent anything untoward—a large-scale political demonstration, for example—from disrupting the games.

The real test, however, will come not in the summer of 2008, but in the year or two after all the visitors go home. How many of the changes in China's political system hinted at on the eve of the Olympics will actually be implemented? How much of the predictable Beijing spring of 2008 will last until 2009 or 2010?

WHO'S INTEGRATING WHOM?

America has been operating with the wrong paradigm for China. Day after day, American officials carry out policies based upon premises about China's future that are at best questionable and at worst downright false.

America's failure of imagination on China is comparable in some ways to its inability to come to grips with terrorism. In both instances, the main obstacle has been conceptual in nature. In the aftermath of the September 11 attacks, it became evident that the George W. Bush administration had devoted virtually all its attention overseas to the task of coping with threats from conventional states, such as North Korea, and had failed to recognize the threat from what are called "nonstate actors"—that is, transnational organizations such as al-Qaeda. This obsession with conventional states amounted to the wrong paradigm.

With China, the conceptual error the United States is making is in the opposite direction. This time, the failure lies not in America's inability to detect an important change, such as the rise of al-Qaeda (I am specifically *not* arguing, as do some on the political

Right, that China will turn into some unimaginable military threat to the United States in the future).

On the contrary, in the case of China the mistake lies simply in the very assumption that change is coming. America hasn't thought much about what it might mean for the United States and the rest of the world to have a repressive, one-party state in China three decades from now, because it is widely assumed that China's political system is destined for far-reaching transformation—that China is destined for a political liberalization, leading eventually to democracy. Yet while China will certainly be a richer and more powerful country a quarter century from now, it could still be an autocracy of one form or another. Its leadership (the Communist Party or whatever it calls itself in the future) may not be willing to tolerate organized political opposition any more than it does today. That is a prospect with profound implications for America and the rest of the world. And it is a prospect that our current paradigm of an inevitably changing China cannot seem to envision.

The paradigm of a China on the road to political liberalization took hold in the United States because it has served certain specific interests within American society. At first, in the late 1970s and 1980s, this idea benefited America's national security establishment. At the time, the United States was seeking close cooperation with China against the Soviet Union, so that the Soviet Union would have to worry about both America and China at once; it was convenient for the Pentagon to make sure the Soviet Union tied down large numbers of troops along the Sino-Soviet border that might otherwise have been deployed in Europe. Amid the ideological struggles of the cold war, cooperation with China's Communist regime was politically touchy in Washington. So the notion that China was in the process of opening up its political system helped smooth the way with Congress and the American public.

In the 1990s, after the Soviet collapse, the paradigm of a politically changing China attracted a new constituency, in some ways more powerful than the Pentagon: the business community. As trade and investment in China became ever more important, American companies (and their counterparts in Europe and Japan) found themselves repeatedly beset with questions about why they were doing business with such a repressive regime, one that had so recently ordered tanks to fire at unarmed citizens. The paradigm of inevitable change offered multinational corporations the answer they needed. Not only was China destined to open up its political system, but—so the theology held—trade would be the key that would unlock the door. Trade would lead to political liberalization and to democracy. The trouble is, the entire paradigm may turn out to be wrong.

■ ■ ■

What should America's strategy be for dealing with China's Leninist regime? The United States currently has what amounts to an official dogma. If you ask America's established political leaders, foreign policy experts, or sinologists what the United States should do about China, you will undoubtedly get some version or another of this approach. It is called "the strategy of integration."

The United States, it is said, should try to integrate the Chinese leadership into the international community. It should seek to help China gain admission to the world's leading international organizations. According to this logic, after China becomes a member of bodies such as the World Trade Organization (which it has now joined), the nature of the regime will change. China's Communist Party leadership will gradually, over time, behave more like other governments; it will become more open in dealing with the Chinese people and with the rest of the world. Richard Haass, president of the Council on Foreign Relations, has written of "the existing opportunity to integrate China into a U.S.-led world order."[1]

This strategy of integration dates back to the Clinton administration. In 1994, after President Clinton abandoned his attempt to use trade as a lever for improving human rights in China, he and his administration needed to divert attention from this embarrassing reversal. They did not wish to concede that they had just downgraded the cause of human rights in China; instead, they sought a new, positive-sounding description of their policy. "Integration" gradually became the label of choice, invoked by the president and his top advisers in press conference after press conference. Integration became, above all, the justification for unrestricted trade with China. "We believe it's the best way to integrate China further into the family of nations and to secure our interests and our ideals," declared Clinton in one typical speech.[2]

George W. Bush and his advisers, without ever admitting they were doing so, perpetuated most of the essentials of Clinton's China policy, including the avowed commitment to integration. During Bush's second term, both Secretary of State Condoleezza Rice and former deputy secretary of state Robert Zoellick have given speeches about China that have called for integrating China into the international community.

"Integration" has thus become another catchphrase like "engagement," the earlier slogan for America's China policy, which originated during the administration of George H. W. Bush. The connotations of the two words are slightly different. Stripped of its pretensions, "engagement" simply meant that America's top leaders should keep on meeting with Chinese leaders (even if nothing ever happened as a result of those meetings). "Integration" means that the United States should not only talk with the Chinese leadership on its own, but also bring it into meetings with other governments and international organizations.

Despite the slightly different connotations, these two words have the same constituency within the United States: Those among America's elite who favor engagement also favor integration, and vice versa. With both words, the suggestion is the same: With enough engagement, with sufficiently vigorous integration, the United States may succeed in altering the nature of the Chinese regime—although it is not clear exactly how this is supposed to happen. In a way, the American approach is a bit patronizing to China: It sounds as if the United States is a weary, experienced trainer bringing China to a diplomatic version of obedience school.

■ ■ ■

The fundamental problem with this strategy of integration is that it raises the obvious question "Who's integrating whom?" Is the United States now integrating China into a new international economic order based upon free market principles? Or, on the other hand, is China now integrating the United States into a new international political order where democracy is no longer favored and where a government's continuing eradication of all organized political opposition is accepted or ignored?

This is not merely a government issue. Private companies—including Internet firms like Yahoo!, Google, and Microsoft—often use slogans like "engagement" and "integration" to explain why they have decided to do business in China, despite Chinese rules and laws that allow continuing censorship. "I think [the Internet] is contributing to Chinese political engagement," Bill Gates told one business gathering.[3] Yet if Microsoft is altering its rules to accommodate China, once again the question is, who's changing whom?

If the world ends up thirty years from now with a Chinese regime that is still a deeply repressive one-party state but is nevertheless a member of the international community in good standing, will that have been a success for the U.S. policy of integration? If so, that same China will serve as a model for dictators, juntas, and other undemocratic governments throughout the world—and, in all likelihood, a leading supporter of these regimes. China is already serving that function with respect to a number of dictatorships, from Burma to Zimbabwe. Thus, when America's leading officials and CEOs speak so breezily of integrating China into the international community, listeners should ask questions such as: If China remains unchanged, what sort of international community will that be? Will it favor the right to dissent? Will it protect freedom of expression? Or will it simply protect free trade and the right to invest?

But wait, say the defenders of America's existing China policy. *We believe in democracy, too. There is no real disagreement here on our ultimate goals. This is all just a question of tactics.* The strategy of integration (or of engagement), its proponents say, is designed to change China's political system and, over the long term, to end its one-party state.

These arguments sound in some ways similar to claims made by Chinese leaders themselves. Because Chinese Communist Party leaders don't like to acknowledge that they intend to maintain their monopoly on power, they sometimes tell visitors that they, too, believe in democracy, that this is the ultimate goal for China, and that it is all merely a question of timing. These claims are designed for the hopelessly gullible; by its actions, day after day, the regime makes clear its tenacious hostility to the idea of political pluralism in China.

Generally, the U.S. proponents of a strategy of integration are not so cynical. To be sure, a few of them may be antidemocratic; there have always been Americans who admire, even revere, the simplicity and convenience of autocracy. However, other proponents of integration seem to believe quite sincerely that if the United States continues its current approach toward China, eventually Chinese leaders will be willing to abandon the monopoly on political power they have maintained since 1949. Yet they fail to explain how or why, under the current American strategy, China's political system will change.

The approaches they have used so far have served to divert attention from the core issue of China's one-party state. The promotion of village elections has proved to be largely unsuccessful, both because the Chinese leadership can confine this experiment exclusively to the villages and because in the villages themselves, authorities have resorted to a variety of methods, including the use of violence, to forestall democracy.

Nor is there evidence that the American drive for promotion of the rule of law will by itself transform the political system. As long as there is no independent judiciary and China remains a one-party regime in which judges are selected by the Communist Party leadership, promoting the rule of law won't bring about fundamental change. Instead, it may lead simply to a more thoroughly legalized system of repression. Indeed, those lawyers in China who attempt to use the judicial system to challenge the Communist Party or to defend the rights of political dissidents have often themselves been subject to persecution, including prison or loss of their jobs.[4]

The strongest impetus for establishment of the rule of law comes from the corporations and investors that are putting their money into China. They need established procedures for resolving financial disputes, just as companies and investors require everywhere else in the world. It is in the interest of the Chinese regime to keep the investment dollars, euros, and yen flowing into the country, so Chinese officials are willing to establish some judicial procedures for the foreign companies. However, the result could well be a Chinese legal system that offers special protection for foreign investors but not to ordinary Chinese individuals, much less to targets of the regime such as political dissidents or Tibetan activists.

And that raises the larger question about America's current strategy of integration. Whom does it benefit? Above all, it enriches the elites in both China and the United States. The strategy is good for the American business community, which gets to trade with China and invest in China. And integration is at least equally good for the new class emerging in Chinese cities—the managers and entrepreneurs, many of them former party cadres or the relatives of cadres, who are getting rich from the booming trade and investment in China.

America's China policy has not been nearly so beneficial for working-class Americans—particularly the tens of thousands who have lost their jobs in the United States as the end result of the policy of integration. The American people were told many years ago that bringing China into the international economic system would help change the Chinese political system. Now, American workers may well begin to wonder whether this argument was merely a cruel hoax. Nor has the strategy of integration been such a blessing for ordinary Chinese. To be sure, China as a whole is more prosperous than it has ever been in the past, but this new prosperity is enjoyed mostly by the urban middle class, not by its overworked, underpaid factory workers or by the hundreds of millions of peasants in the countryside.

Indeed, it is precisely because the regime knows how restive and disenchanted the Chinese people are that it refuses to open up to any form of democracy. The Chinese leaders know that if there were elections, they could be thrown out of office. Although they regularly accuse foreigners of hurting "the feelings of the Chinese people," they do not want to establish any voting system that would permit an impartial assessment of the feelings of the Chinese people toward their own government. Democracy, or even an organization calling for future democracy, is a threat to the existing political and economic order in China. That is why the regime continues to repress all forms of organized dissent and political opposition. And that is why China's new class of managers and executives, who profit from keeping wages low, supports the regime in its ongoing repression.

■ ■ ■

The underlying premise of the American proponents of integration is that we can put off until many years from now the question of

Chinese democracy. Let China develop, so goes the argument; let the country get richer; let it be integrated into organizations like the World Trade Organization; and then, two or three decades from now, it may be a more advantageous time to try to push hard for China to open up its political system.

But this issue of timing is not as simple as the proponents would claim. Two or three decades from now, it may be too late. By then China will be wealthier, and the entrenched interests opposing democracy will probably be much stronger. By then China will be so thoroughly integrated into the world's financial and diplomatic systems, because of its sheer commercial power, that there will be no international support for any movement to open up China's political system.

Sometimes, in dealing with China, sooner is better than later. There have been instances in the past when the United States devised policies that, whatever their merits, failed because they were out-of-date. One classic example was the American attempt in 1993–1994 to make the renewal of China's annual trade benefits conditional upon specific improvements in human rights. That particular idea had its origins in the year after China's epochal crackdown on the Tiananmen demonstrations. And indeed, at the time, this tactic might have had a better chance; in 1989–1991, the Chinese economy was fragile—unimaginably so, by current standards. China's principal international loans had been temporarily suspended, and China's growth rate, for a time, was negligible. By the time the Clinton administration took office in 1993, the Chinese economy had recovered and was growing at a remarkable rate. Business executives, prime ministers, and presidents were rushing to Beijing in hopes of landing contracts. By then the situation in China had changed, and the American attempt at trade linkage was doomed to failure.

The point is that the best time to try to forestall the emergence of a permanent Chinese autocracy may well be now or in the next few years—not a quarter century from now, when the regime and the current system of modernized, business-supported repression could well be vastly more established and entrenched.

■ ■ ■

What should the United States do to encourage democratic change in China? A detailed list of policies can emerge only after we rid ourselves of the delusions and false assumptions upon which our China policy has long been based.

Above all, we have to stop taking it for granted that China is heading inevitably for political liberalization and democracy. George W. Bush has continued to repeat the American mantra about China every bit as much as did his predecessors. "As China reforms its economy, its leaders are finding that once the door to freedom is opened even a crack, it cannot be closed," Bush declared in one typical speech. Such words convey a heartwarming sense of hopefulness about China but do not match the reality of China itself, where doors are regularly opened by more than a crack and then closed again. America's political and corporate leaders also need to stop spreading the lie that trade will bring an end to China's one-party political system. This fiction has been skillfully employed, over and over again, to help win the support of Congress and the American public for approval of trade with China. Trade is trade. It is not a magic political potion for democracy. Its benefits and costs are in the economic sphere; trade has not brought an end to political repression or the Chinese Communist Party's monopoly on power, and there is not the slightest reason to think it will do so in the future, either. In fact, it is possible that our trade with China is merely helping its autocratic regime to become richer and more powerful. America's current China policy amounts to an unstated bargain: We have abandoned any serious attempt to challenge China's one-party state, and we have gotten in exchange the right to unfettered commerce with China.

What we need now, above all, are political leaders who are willing to challenge America's stale logic and phraseology concerning China. We need politicians who will call attention to the fact that America has been carrying out a policy that benefits business interests in both the United States and China far more than it helps ordinary working people in either country.

The reexamination should apply to both political parties and to both poles of the ideological spectrum. On the Democratic Left, we need people who will question the assumptions that it is somehow "progressive" to say that democracy doesn't matter or to assume that it will automatically come to China someday. Such views aren't in the least progressive, liberal, or enlightened. Rather, they were developed by the Clinton administration to justify policies that would enable Bill Clinton to win corporate support. There were, during the 1990s, other views concerning China within the Democratic Party—those of Nancy Pelosi, for example, and George Mitchell, who took strong stands on behalf of human rights in China. The Democrats rejected those alternative approaches a decade ago but should reexamine them now.

Within the Republican Party, we need political leaders willing to challenge the Business Roundtable mentality that has dominated the party's thinking on China for so long. If Republicans really care about political freedom, why should they allow American policy toward China to be dominated by corporate interests, while the world's most populous country is governed by a single party that permits no political opposition? George W. Bush was able to conceal his business-oriented approach to China behind a facade of hawkish rhetoric. Republicans should not allow this to happen again.

Once America finally recognizes that China is *not* moving inevitably toward democracy, we can begin to decide what the right approach should be. On the one hand, it is possible that America may seek new measures to goad the Chinese leadership toward democratic change. America also might want to reconsider its doctrinaire adherence to free trade in dealing with China.

Alternatively, it's possible the American people may decide that there's absolutely nothing the United States can or should do about a huge, permanently undemocratic, enduringly repressive China. As described in this book, such an entity, a Chinese autocracy persisting into the mid-twenty-first century, would cause large problems for American policy elsewhere in the world. Nevertheless, after weighing the costs and benefits of trying to push for democracy in China, America could opt for a policy of sheer acceptance of the existing order.

The American people are not being given such options now, because the choices are not being laid out. There is virtually no public debate about the Third Scenario. American politicians of both parties talk regularly as if liberalization and democracy are eventually coming to China—that is, that China will follow the Soothing Scenario. Or, occasionally, they raise the prospect of political upheaval in China, the Upheaval Scenario. But the Third Scenario? At the moment, that seems to be outside our public discourse. We need to think about it in order to figure out what we want to do.

I have never written a book in which I hoped so fervently that I would be proved wrong. It would be heartening if China's leaders proceed along the lines that America's political leaders predict. It would be wonderful if China opened up, either gradually or suddenly, to a new political system in which the country's 1.3 billion people are given a chance to choose their own leaders. While wishing for such an outcome, I will not hold my breath.

AFTERWORD

This book was first published at the beginning of 2007. I have no reason to believe that Chinese leader Hu Jintao has read it or even knows of its existence; he has many other demands on his time. Yet in the months after the book came out, it seemed almost as though Hu and the rest of China's Communist Party leadership had embarked on a concerted campaign to confirm the central thesis of *The China Fantasy*: that China is not headed for democracy or for any far-reaching political liberalization.

The Soothing Scenario put forward by American political and business leaders—that trade and investment will liberalize China's political system—seemed ever more unlikely. Instead, in early 2007, Hu and his aides were laying the groundwork for the Third Scenario. They made clear that in the coming years China will expand its economic interaction with the rest of the world, but will also remain a one-party state that prohibits organized political opposition to the Chinese Communist Party.

In June 2007, Hu gathered together the leading cadres from China's provinces and municipalities for a speech he delivered at the Central Party School, the institution that is in charge of doctrine, strategy and planning for the Chinese Communist Party. It was a rare occasion: the entire Politburo Standing Committee, all of China's most senior leaders, were present. Hu Jintao broke new sartorial ground at this event: he spoke in an open-collared white shirt and casual trousers, forsaking the business suit that Chinese leaders have been accustomed to wearing in recent years.

Hu's political message, however, was as cautious and conservative as a charcoal gray suit. His speech represented, in many ways, a repetition of the jargon of the past. He emphasized that the Chinese Communist Party will continue to maintain its monopoly on political power. Any reforms in China "must adhere to the correct political orientation," Hu said. "We must uphold the party's leadership, make the people the masters of the country, rule the country by law, and bring the three into organic harmony; and we must continue to push forward the self-improvement and self-development of our socialist political system."[1]

The reader should particularly take note of Hu's words that the Communist Party will rule the country "*by* law." He did not say *under* law, or that the leadership would obey the rule *of* law. This is a significant distinction. In other words, the party remains in charge of the judicial system, and the law will be used on behalf of the party.

Since the original publication of The China Fantasy, Chinese leaders have also reaffirmed that judges and the court system are not independent but will remain under party control. "There is no question about where legal departments should stand. The correct political stand is where the party stands," said Luo Gan, the member of the Politburo Standing Committee in charge of internal security and the judiciary, in a speech last February. The same principles hold for China's prosecutors and police. "All law-enforcement activities should be led by the party," Luo asserted. "All reform measures should be conducive to the socialist system and the strengthening of the party leadership." Luo warned that "enemy forces" were seeking to use China's courts and legal system to "divide our country."[2]

Nor have the signs been encouraging for the development of an independent civil society in China. Those who hope for political liberalization argue that it will come only after an emerging middle class begins to develop nongovernment organizations that can operate without ties to the government or the ruling party. The Chinese leadership, however, continues to view independent groups as a threat to the Communist Party's monopoly on power, and it seems determined to restrict the growth of such groups. That was the message it delivered by closing down a serious, respected newsletter called *China Development Brief*.

For more than a decade, starting in 1996, *China Development Brief* had sought to report on the growth of civil society in China. It had served as a source of information about issues such as the environment, women's health and rural issues. It audience included officials of the United Nations and the World Bank, and members of Chinese nongovernment organizations. In June 2007, a dozen Beijing security and municipal officials raided the offices of *China Development Brief* and closed it down on the grounds that it had been conducting "unauthorized" surveys. Nick Young, the founder of the publication, acknowledged afterward that China had proved to be less tolerant than he had previously believed. "I have spent the last decade telling foreigners that China is not as repressive and totalitarian as Western media often portray it to be," he said. "At the end of the day, I hoped that if we had an open, intelligence conversation, we would be accepted. But I think we miscalculated, or they miscalculated."[3]

Those Chinese who were willing to speak out against the regime continued to find that they were invariably unable to organize inside China and that they often could not travel outside the country, either. In July 2007, Jiang Yanyong, the retired People's Liberation Army physician who exposed the cover-up of SARS in China and condemned the regime's decision to use military force against the Tiananmen Square demonstrations (see page 16), was given a human rights award by the New York Academy of Sciences. The regime refused to allow him to go to the United States.

In the spring of 2007, Amnesty International, the London-based human rights organization, concluded that China was continuing to detain political activists without trial, to tighten controls on Chinese journalists and to expel unwanted people from the streets of Beijing in preparation for the Olympic Games. The State Department's annual human rights report in 2007 asserted that China has become the world's leader in censoring and controlling the Internet.[4]

∎ ∎ ∎

On July 10, 2007, China executed Zheng Xiaoyu, the former head of the country's State Food and Drug Administration. The Supreme People's Court had imposed the death sentence after finding that Zheng accepted more than $800,000 in bribes from pharmaceutical companies to approve medicines that turned out to be fakes. At least ten people in China reportedly died from one of these medicines, a spurious antibiotic.

Zheng's execution came in the wake of a growing international furor about the safety of Chinese products. Over the previous few weeks, there had been a wave of revelations in the United States and elsewhere about contaminated or defective Chinese goods, including pet food, tires, toys, toothpaste and shellfish. Chinese authorities were worried that these stories could cause lasting damage to the reputation of Chinese exports. One part of China's response to the contamination scandals was to seek to limit the press coverage, both inside China and overseas. "I think it would be better if the media would stop playing up this issue," Qin Gang, a foreign ministry spokesman, told reporters.[5]

The product-safety scandals pointed once again to the problems posed by China's political system, both for the rest of the world and for the Chinese people themselves. Under the current system, there can be no independent consumer movement in China, no Chinese version of Ralph Nader or of Germany's Green Party.

Substandard goods are often produced by local factories, which have close, sometimes corrupt relationships with local Communist Party officials. The officials cannot be voted out of office and have the power to retaliate against those who seek to expose them. It was telling that one year earlier, a local Chinese pharmaceutical employee was jailed for several months after he had merely posted an Internet essay (written by someone else) about Zheng's corruption.[6]

Some observers pointed out that the authorities in Beijing lack the means to control quality standards on manufactured goods throughout the country. By this argument, the central government is generally weak and cannot scrutinize what the many thousands of local factories are producing. "The government has a limited ability to enforce things," one World Health Organization representative explained. Thus, the execution of Zheng, dramatic and harsh as it was, masked the larger trend of lax enforcement.

As a description of where China stands today, this analysis is probably accurate. However, it also raises secondary questions. The regime seems to be able to enforce its will, even at the local level, when it comes to political opposition. Why are authorities in Beijing so effective in forestalling organized dissent, but so powerless when it comes to preventing corruption or defective goods? One answer is that China maintains a huge internal-security apparatus to deal with the former, but not the latter. Why can't some of the Chinese Ministry of State Security's numerous watchers and eavesdroppers be reassigned to problems like bribery and counterfeit goods? Apparently because of fears that the Communist Party's control of the country would be in jeopardy if there were not so many people assigned to internal security. The product-safety scandals, then, serve to illustrate the underlying nature of the Chinese regime.

■ ■ ■

In sum, China now seems to be headed in the opposite direction from what the proponents of the Soothing Scenario have predicted. While continuing to expand its economy and trade and investment ties with the rest of the world, the regime has not liberalized its political system. For Chinese leaders, the country's rapidly-growing economy has become a rationale for preserving the status quo.

This is not the path American leaders or experts thought China would take a decade ago. In 1996, at a conference at Stanford University on "China and World Affairs in 2010," one of America's most prominent and experienced China scholars, Michel Oksenberg, forecast that the Chinese Communist Party would within fifteen years adopt some of the trappings of an electoral system—one it could then dominate like, say, Japan's Liberal Democratic Party. "I am tempted to suggest that China's paramount leader will (by 2010) have either been directly elected or selected via an elected, multi-party national parliament," Oksenberg told the conference. He argued that China would follow the path taken by Japan, Taiwan and South Korea from market economy to political openings to democracy. "The outside world and the porousness of China's borders will make it difficult for China's leaders to resist those trends."[7]

As it turns out, China does seem to be resisting those trends. The prediction by Bill Clinton that China was on the wrong side of history now seems out of date. Perhaps history is on China's side. Its leadership is showing that a regime can forestall organized political opposition for an extended period of time and can at the same time achieve high rates of economic growth. The Chinese middle class shows no particular eagerness for political pluralism. Instead, China seems to be emerging as the model for an enduring, prosperous authoritarianism.

■ ■ ■

And what has been the response of American elites? As it grows ever
more evident that the Chinese leadership will seek to preserve the essentials of the current one-party state, how do American leaders explain away China's continuing repression of all organized opposition?
To answer that, one must explore a series of new excuses and eu-
phemisms that have begun to take hold among the American elite.

In May 2007, the Council on Foreign Relations—the presti-
gious private group, based in New York, which includes America's
most influential figures in international affairs—released the results
of a study by an independent task force on China. The report rec-
ommended the same general approaches as in the past: America
should carry out a policy of engagement with China and should
aim at "integrating China into the international community."[8] (The
proponents of "integration" did not address the more awkward questions: Who is integrating whom? While the United States prides itself on bringing China into the current international system it now
dominates, is China meanwhile integrating the United States into a
new order in which authoritarianism is respectable?)

At a New York press conference after the report was released, a
Time magazine correspondent asked Carla Hills, the co-chair of
the task force, about a problem: Over the past couple of years, the
reporter said, one could argue that political repression in China
had been increasing. Was there some point at which China might
become "so authoritarian and so repressive" that Hills would no
longer recommend policies of "engagement" or "integration"?

Hills's first response was to offer an updated version of what I
have called the "Cultural Revolution baseline" (see page 75), one of
the most frequent rationalizations for Chinese repression—that is, to
explain away current repression by arguing that things are better
than they were in the past. Hills said she had been visiting China for
nearly three decades and that the country had changed dramatically

since then. The reporter gently posed once again his original question: "I was really thinking of the last couple of years," he said.

Hills shifted ground. She noted that China's current leaders have recently been making efforts to alleviate rural poverty, to ease tax burdens on the Chinese people, and to eliminate corruption. She came to her conclusion: "What there hasn't been is American-style democracy," she asserted.[9]

"American-style democracy" is a phrase worthy of further scrutiny. I have found that in some of the discussions provoked by the publication of The China Fantasy, these same words have come up from time to time. Those who criticize Chinese repression are not infrequently accused of seeking to impose American-style democracy on China. Indeed, the phrase could well be added to the Lexicon of Dismissal described in chapter two.

Note that Hills's questioner had not merely asked her about American-style democracy. He had asked about repression of dissent. At the time of the press conference, Amnesty International, which is not an American organization, had just reported that the human rights climate in China was in some ways getting worse, not better. Nor is there any advocacy of American-style democracy in The China Fantasy. (I would be delighted if China were to move toward a Canadian-style democracy, or a South Korean-style democracy, or a French-style democracy.)

The phrase that Hills employed, "American-style democracy," implies that China has some other form of democracy—one that is, however, not American. This is of course plain wrong, unless, by some Orwellian logic, one alters the definition of that word to mean the opposite of what it has always meant. Hills did not wish to say that there has been no democracy in China, and so she added the adjective, "American-style."

Inside China, the phrase serves the additional diversionary purpose of suggesting that the country's authoritarian regime represents a form of resistance to the foreign policies of the United States. But this is absurd. Lots of countries around the world maintain lively democracies while also remaining independent of American foreign policy. At the time of the Bush administration's invasion of Iraq, the country that led the opposition at the United Nations was France, a democracy. China's authoritarian regime was much more cautious.

"American-style democracy" is one of several phrases in the emerging new vocabulary used to rationalize the perpetuation of China's one-party system. Another is the phrase "humane governance." A prominent American specialist on China, David Lampton, recently voiced the hope that China is moving to "more humane governance domestically and more cooperative behavior internationally."[10] Such careful wording seeks to deflect questions about the nature of China's political system: for example, whether there will ever be any organized political opposition or freedom of the press. The phrase "more humane governance" seems to imply that what counts is not whether China's political system will change, but rather whether its leaders will become more benevolent.

Another diversionary word offered by the Chinese Communist Party is "participation." "We must continue to expand orderly political participation of our citizens," Chinese leader Hu Jintao told party officials in his speech to the Central Party School in May 2007.[11] Of course, although Hu did not have to say it, one can have "participation" while still preserving a one-party system and banning all opposition. Other Chinese officials have begun to speak of the possibility of "inner-party democracy"—some sort of process for allowing Communist Party officials to choose their own leaders. This could well represent a step forward for the party itself, but would of course leave the 1.2 billion Chinese who are not party members without any say in how their country is governed.

■   ■   ■

The use of phrases such as "humane governance" raises an interesting question: Is there some point at which American elites will stop claiming that trade with China will liberalize its political system? Will our leaders shift course and, rather than arguing that the United States is changing China, instead contend that we must accept China's one-party state as a lasting reality? In short, will the China Fantasy eventually be abandoned?

There are some signs that American elites are becoming more guarded in what they forecast for China. No longer do political leaders, business executives or scholars assert so readily that China is destined for far-reaching political change. The 2007 report by the Council on Foreign Relations acknowledged there was "no evidence to suggest that China is planning to pursue significant democratic reforms in the near term." It warned against the idea that "a more democratic system will inevitably emerge in China because of 'inexorable tides.'"[12]

It might be argued that the China Fantasy was suited to a particular time and served a particular purpose, one that is no longer as necessary as it once was. During the 1990s, American and multinational corporations were repeatedly threatened by the possibility that Congress might restrict trade with China, at a time when it was becoming not only a crucial market but the world's fastest-growing economy. The American public had been shocked by China's bloody crackdown on the demonstrations at Tiananmen Square and elsewhere in China. The ideas that China was destined for political liberalization, and that trade would help open up the country's political system, helped to preserve business with China during this tumultuous period.

Since then, China has been admitted to the World Trade Organization, and its continued trade relations with the United States are no longer subject to congressional review. Commerce with China is no longer in doubt. As a result, American elites no longer find it so useful to make extravagant claims about China's future or about the liberalizing effects of trade. Instead, American leaders are more willing to concede that China's political system is not destined for change.

Nevertheless, I think the China Fantasy will persist. Whenever there is a need for public or congressional support for American policies toward China, our leaders will continue to suggest that the policies in question are helping to open up China. The opposite possibility—that, in fact, trade and investment with China are helping to perpetuate the one-party system—is still not politically acceptable in the United States.

The aim of this book has been to question assumptions about China's future. Americans in particular like to believe that they are changing China and that the Chinese people are becoming Americanized. That has been true throughout much of American history, and it remains true today. These assumptions have never been borne out in the past, and I doubt they will prove to be true in the years to come.

Washington, D.C.
August 1, 2007

ACKNOWLEDGMENTS

I was fortunate to have had the support of two extraordinary institutions while writing this book. The first was Johns Hopkins University's Paul H. Nitze School of Advanced International Studies (SAIS), where I have been based as author in residence beginning in 2004. The second was the American Academy in Berlin, where I lived as a fellow for four months in the fall of 2005. Both institutions provided the research help and the vibrant intellectual climate necessary for writing a book. At SAIS, I am especially grateful to Dean Jessica Einhorn; to Thomas Keaney, the executive director of the Foreign Policy Institute; and to Courtney Mata, the FPI's ever-helpful administrator. At the American Academy, special thanks go to executive director Gary Smith, who understands what writers need and how they think.

This book, like my previous one *Rise of the Vulcans*, would not have come into being without the help of Adrian Zackheim, my editor at Viking, and Rafe Sagalyn, my agent. They recognized how much I wanted to write this book and created the opportunity to do it. As always, several people assisted by reading the manuscript, or parts of it, and offering their thoughts. Among them were Warren I. Cohen, the leading historian of America's relations with China, and of course my wife, Caroline; daughter, Elizabeth; and son, Theodore.

None of the institutions or the people who helped so much in producing the book are responsible for the views expressed here, which represent solely my own long-considered ideas.

NOTES

CHAPTER ONE: THE THIRD SCENARIO

1. Governor George W. Bush, "A Distinctly American Internationalism," speech at Ronald Reagan Presidential Library, Simi Valley, Calif., Nov. 19, 1999.
2. Transcript of President Bill Clinton's press conference with Jiang Zemin, Jan. 28, 1997.
3. "U.K.'s Blair Says Democracy in China Is Unstoppable," Bloomberg News Service, Sept. 6, 2005.
4. See State Department Country Reports on Human Rights Practices, 2005, www.state.gov/g/drl/hrrpt/2005/61605.htm.
5. Edward Cody, "Chinese Activists Targeted by Thug Violence," *Washington Post*, Jan. 1, 2006, p. A-14; State Department Country Reports.
6. Jim Yardley, "Democracy, Chinese Style: 2 Steps Forward, 1 Step Back," *New York Times*, Dec. 21, 2003, section 1, p. 3. For other uses of "two steps forward," see Elisabeth Rosenthal, "Beijing in a Rear-Guard Battle Against a Newly Spirited Press," *New York Times*, Sept. 15, 2002, p. 1; "Deng's Two-Step: Two Steps Forward, One Back," *New York Times*, Jan. 30, 1987, p. A-26.

7. Kevin Platt, "Clinton's First China Stop Loaded with Spin," *Christian Science Monitor*, June 25, 1998, p. 1.

8. Gerald Segal, "The Muddle Kingdom?: China's Changing Shape," *Foreign Affairs* (May–June 1994): 43.

9. Gordon G. Chang, *The Coming Collapse of China* (New York: Random House, 2001), pp. xvi, xix.

10. For the George H. W. Bush administration, see James Mann, *About Face* (New York: Alfred A. Knopf, 1998), p. 228. For the Clinton administration, see transcript of Samuel Berger remarks to Woodrow Wilson International Center, Feb. 2, 2000.

11. Warren I. Cohen, *America's Response to China*, 4th ed. (New York: Columbia University Press, 1990), p. 242.

12. I am speaking here, of course, of the parts of the country where Chinese is the main written language. The histories of Tibet and Xinjiang are different.

13. See "Warning over Unrest After Violent Protests," *South China Morning Post*, July 29, 2005, quoting *People's Daily* of July 28, 2005.

14. Vivien Pik-Kwan Chan, "Propaganda Tag Axed in Image Facelift," *South China Morning Post*, May 12, 1998, p. 7.

15. See Cohen, *America's Response to China*, p. 179.

16. Richard N. Haass, *The Opportunist* (New York: Public Affairs, 2005), pp. 152–53.

17. Thomas L. Friedman, *The Lexus and the Olive Tree* (New York: Anchor Books, 2000), p. 183.

18. See Philip P. Pan, "China Frees SARS Hero," *Washington Post*, July 25, 2004, p. A-3. Jiang was subsequently kept under house arrest for eight months.

19. In September 2005, Chinese premier Wen Jiabao suggested in a BBC interview that China might at some point allow elections at the township level. But the Chinese government weeks later issued a white paper on democracy that took no steps toward township elections and defined China as a "democratic dictatorship," in which the Communist Party would play the leading role. See Jonathan Watts, "Chinese Communists Dash Hopes of Democratic Reform," *The Guardian*, Oct. 21, 2005, p. 19.

20. See, for example, Edward Cody, "In Chinese Uprisings, Peasants Find New Allies," *Washington Post*, Nov. 26, 2005, p. 1.

21. See John Pomfret, "In Rural China, Democracy Not All It Seems," *Washington Post*, Aug. 26, 2000, page A-1; Josephine Ma, "Create a

Uniform System for Village Polls, Says Jimmy Carter," *South China Morning Post*, Sept. 9, 2003, p. 5; "Carter: China Village Vote Gives Democracy a Boost," *Atlanta Journal-Constitution*, Sept. 6, 2001, p. 1-B.

22. Hu Jintao speech to APEC CEO conference, Nov. 19, 2005.

23. The theory dates back to Immanuel Kant. For recent discussions, see Aaron L. Friedberg, "The Future of U.S.-China Relations: Is Conflict Inevitable?" *International Security* 30, no. 2 (Fall 2005): 15; and Gary J. Bass, "Are Democracies Really More Peaceful?" *New York Times Magazine*, Jan. 1, 2006, p. 18.

24. "China to Update Mugabe Spy Net," *The Australian*, May 20, 2005, p. 12.

25. See Andrew Higgins, "Chinese Joy Recedes as the Tide Turns," *The Independent*, Aug. 23, 1991, p. 7.

26. Samuel R. Berger, "A Foreign Policy for the Global Age," *Foreign Affairs*, 79, no. 6 (November–December 2000): 28–29.

CHAPTER TWO: THE LEXICON OF DISMISSAL

1. See "But Not That," editorial, *Washington Post*, July 3, 1987.

2. See "China Revalues the Yuan," *New York Times*, July 22, 2005; and "No Way to Treat a Dragon," *New York Times*, Aug. 4, 2005.

3. Tom Plate, "Twin Stars Shone over 2005," *South China Morning Post*, Dec. 31, 2005, p. 11.

4. See Warren P. Strobel, "Powell Lauds Panama for Progress Towards Democracy," Knight Ridder News Service, Nov. 4, 2003; "A Human Rights Defender," *San Francisco Chronicle*, Dec. 13, 2001, p. A24.

5. John Fraser, *The Chinese* (New York: Summit Books, 1980), p. 201.

6. See Robert J. Samuelson, "China's Oil Bid," *Washington Post*, July 6, 2005, p. A-17.

7. David M. Lampton, "Paradigm Lost: The Demise of 'Weak China,'" *National Interest* (Fall 2005): 69.

8. See, for example, A. Doak Barnett, "Ten Years After Mao," *Foreign Affairs* (Fall 1986): 37.

9. One of the former U.S. officials who had taken part in the Nixon-Kissinger opening to China, Roger Sullivan, resigned from his position as head of the U.S.-China Business Council because he could no longer justify working with the regime after the Tiananmen crackdown.

10. Robert Kaiser and Steven Mufson, "'Blue Team' Draws a Hard Line on Beijing," *Washington Post*, Feb. 22, 2000, p. A-1.

CHAPTER THREE: THE STARBUCKS FALLACY

1. Nicholas D. Kristof, "The Tiananmen Victory," *New York Times*, June 2, 2004, p. 19 (italics added).
2. Ibid.
3. Angus Deming et al., "Bearbaiting," *Newsweek*, Feb. 12, 1979, p. 22.
4. Orville Schell, *In the People's Republic* (New York: Random House, 1977), p. viii.
5. David M. Lampton, *Same Bed, Different Dreams: Managing U.S.- China Relations, 1989–2000* (Berkeley: University of California Press, 2001), p. 7.
6. "Xinhua Interviews Clinton Security Advisor Sandy Berger," Foreign Broadcast Information Service, March 17, 2004.
7. See Jeffrey H. Birnbaum, "Taking Costly Counsel from a States- man," *Washington Post*, March 29, 2004, p. E-1.
8. In the spring of 2005, Greenberg was forced by his board to resign as chairman and chief executive of AIG. He continued to serve as the chairman and CEO of two other insurance companies, C.V. Starr and C.V. Starr International, which together control an estimated $22 billion worth of AIG stock. See Jenny Anderson, "In Lawsuit, C.V. Starr Accuses A.I.G. of Hurting Its Business," *New York Times*, Jan. 30, 2006, p. C-1.
9. Maurice R. Greenberg, "On Leadership," *National Interest*, no. 82 (Winter 2005–2006): 25.
10. Steven Mufson, "A Benefactor Flexes His Wallet," *Washington Post*, May 11, 2000, p. A-30.
11. For a full description, see Ross Y. Koen, *The China Lobby in Ameri- can Politics* (New York: Macmillan, 1960).
12. Indeed, it is not accurate now to speak of a "Taiwan lobby," because it is not a single entity. Democratic Taiwan now has competing po- litical parties with different visions of the island's future relationship with China.

CHAPTER FOUR: THE P-FACTOR

1. Quoted from Henry Kissinger memo to Richard Nixon, "My Asian Trip," Feb. 27, 1973, p. 6, in Nixon Collection, National Archives.
2. A more extensive and extremely perceptive explanation of China's approach is contained in Richard H. Solomon, *Chinese Political Negotiating Behavior, 1967–1984* (Santa Monica: Rand Corporation, 1995). This study was originally done for the U.S. intelligence community; it was declassified as a result of a Freedom of Information Act request by the author and the *Los Angeles Times*.
3. See James Mann, *About Face* (New York: Alfred A. Knopf, 1998), p. 101.
4. Ibid., pp. 106–07.
5. See, for example, text of letter from President Bush to the House of Representatives, March 2, 1992.
6. Transcript of President Clinton press conference with Jiang Zemin, Oct. 29, 1998; transcript of President Clinton press conference in Hong Kong, July 4, 1998.
7. Madeleine Albright, address to the Commonwealth Club, San Francisco, June 24, 1997.
8. Remarks by Bill Clinton to the Johns Hopkins University Paul H. Nitze School of Advanced International Studies, March 8, 2000.
9. Text of Bush inaugural speech, Jan. 20, 2005.
10. White House transcript, State of the Union Address by the President, Jan. 31, 2006.
11. Transcript of Bush remarks to the travel pool in China, Nov. 20, 2005; transcript of Bush speech on freedom and democracy in Kyoto, Nov. 16, 2005.

CHAPTER FIVE: LET THE GAMES BEGIN

1. John Pomfret, "China Celebrates Its Fiftieth; Communists' Parade Highlights Military, Political, Economic Might," Oct. 1, 1999, p. A-25.
2. Thomas L. Friedman, "Thou Shalt Not Destroy the Center," *New York Times*, Nov. 11, 2005, p. A-23.
3. See Jonathan Watts, "Satellite Data Reveals Beijing as Air Pollution Capital of World," *The Guardian*, Oct. 31, 2005, p. 22.

CONCLUSION: WHO'S INTEGRATING WHOM?

1. Richard N. Haass, *The Opportunity* (New York: PublicAffairs, 2005), p. 152.
2. Remarks by Bill Clinton to Young Presidents Organization, May 19, 1997.
3. "Gates: Censorship, Software Piracy No Reason Not to Do Business in China," Associated Press, Davos, Switzerland, Jan. 28, 2006.
4. See, for example, Joseph Kahn, "Legal Gadfly Bites Hard, and Beijing Slaps Him," *New York Times*, Dec. 13, 2005, p. 1.

AFTERWORD

1. Text of Hu Jintao speech to Central Party School, June 25, 2007, published by Xinhua news service.
2. Joseph Kahn, "Chinese Official Warns Against Judicial Independence," *New York Times*, Feb. 3, 2007, p. A-5.
3. Peter Ford, "Magazine Covering Civil-Society Groups Is Shut Down in China," *Christian Science Monitor*, July 12, 2007, p. 4; "Message from the Editor," chinadevelopmentbrief.com; Joseph Kahn, "China Orders Western Newsletter to Halt Operations, Editor Says," *New York Times*, July 12, 2007, p. 3.
4. David Pierson, "China Gets Low Grade in Human Rights," *Los Angeles Times*, May 1, 2007, p. A-3; Nora Boustany, "State Department Human Rights Report Faults China's Curbs on Internet," *Washington Post*, March 7, 2007, p. A-10.
5. Jonathan Watts, "Made in China: Tainted Food, Fake Drugs and Dodgy Paint," *The Guardian*, July 5, 2007, p. 21.
6. Aniana Eunjung Cha, "Safety Falters As Chinese Quiet Those Who Cry Foul," *Washington Post*, July 19, 2007, p. A1.
7. Jon Stewart, "Worldview: A Democratic China by 2010?" *San Francisco Chronicle*, May 26, 1996, p. SC-8.
8. "U.S.-China Relations: An Affirmative Agenda, A Responsible Course," Independent Task Force Report No. 59, Council on Foreign Relations, May 2007.

9. Press conference of Council on Foreign Relations Task Force, May 14, 2007.
10. See David M. Lampton, "The Wrong Question," on Foreign Policy Web site, http://www.foreignpolicy.com/story/cms.php?story_id=3837.
11. Text of Hu Jintao speech, *op. cit.*
12. Council on Foreign Relations report, *op. cit.*, pp. 21, 29.

INDEX

Albright, Madeleine, 60, 84, 98
American Enterprise Institute, xi
American International Group (AIG), 62
Asia Society, 62, 64
Association for Asian Studies, xi
Atlantic Council, 62
Aung San Suu Kyi, 24
authoritarian rule, *see* one-party system in China

Bao Tong, 3
Barshefsky, Charlene, 61
Beijing Olympic Games, *see* Olympics Games of 2008, Beijing summer
Berger, Samuel, 9, 26–27, 60, 61
Berlin Wall, fall of the, 8, 26, 78, 83
Blair, Tony, 3
Brookings Institution, xi, 62
Buchanan, Patrick, 58
Burma (Myanmar), 24, 25, 86, 105

Bush, George H. W.,
    administration of, 85
    China policy, 3, 8, 26, 69, 77–80, 81, 104
Bush, George W., administration of
    China policy, 2, 4, 70, 84–88, 104, 110
    democracy as linchpin of foreign policy of, 86–87
    Iraq war, 38, 85
    "nonstate actors" and, 101
Bush, Prescott, Jr., 85
business and financial interests in China, xii, 66–67, 79–80, 110
    Beijing Olympics of 2008 and, 92
Business Roundtable, 64, 111

cabinet members, career paths of, 59–61
capitalism in China, *see* economic liberalization in China; trade with China

Carnegie Endowment for
     International Peace, xi
Carter, Jimmy, 18, 20
     China policy, 42, 71, 74–76
Carter Center, 18, 19
censorship, see dissent in China,
     suppression of; speech,
     freedom of
Central Intelligence Agency
     (CIA), x, 61
Chang, Gordon G., 8
chaos in China and Upheaval
     Scenario, 7–10
Cheney, Dick, 32
Chen Shui-bian, 17, 33, 35
Chiang Ching-kuo, 13
Chiang Kai-shek, 12, 41–42, 56,
     63, 72–73
     Roosevelt administration and,
     97–98
"China bashing" "China basher,"
     30–31, 47
China Daily, 98
China Democratic Party, 98–99
"China hands," U.S. policy and,
     39–46
Chinese Communist Party, see
     one-party system in China
Cisco, 17
Clinton, Bill, administration of,
     26–27, 98–99
     China policy, 2–3, 4, 6, 8–9, 69,
     80–84, 88, 103–4, 111
Cohen, William S., 60
cold war, 23, 26, 32–33, 77, 78,
     82, 102
"cold war mentality," 32–34
Colson, Chuck, 74
Coming Collapse of China, The
     (Chang), 8
Communist Party in China, see
     one-party system in China
Congress, U.S., 26, 81, 84

corporations, see business and
     financial interests in China
corruption in China, 7, 54, 65, 97
Council on Foreign Relations, 62,
     64
Cultural Revolution, 55, 72, 74,
     75, 76
C. V. Starr Foundation, 62
Czechoslovakia, 78

Dalai Lama, 17, 31, 35
Defense Department, U.S., x, 61,
     102
democracy(ies)
     George W. Bush's foreign policy
     and, 86–87
     China's transformation to, see
     political liberalization of
     China
     in East Asia, 12–13, 44, 50–51, 87
     historical record of wars
     between, 22
     "ideological" label, 38–39
     Iraq war, as grounds for, 38
     see also one-party system in
     China
Democracy Wall, Beijing, 15, 36,
     75
Democratic Party, 18
Deng Liqun, 58
Deng Xiaoping, 15, 18, 44, 55, 75,
     77, 79
     Tiananmen crackdown and, xi,
     44, 78
dissent in China, suppression of,
     xii, 3–4, 15–16, 56, 57, 59,
     64, 65, 66, 87, 98–99
     Beijing Olympics of 2008 and,
     95–96
     legal system and, 107
     presidential policy and, 72, 74,
     75, 76, 80–84
due process, 20

Eastern Europe, 75, 78, 83
    Berlin Wall, fall of the, 8, 26,
        78, 83
East Germany, xi, 76, 78
economic liberalization in China,
    5, 44, 76–77
    rural and migrant populations
        and, 56
    Soothing Scenario and, *see*
        Soothing Scenario
    Third Scenario and, 10–13
    see also trade with China
Egypt, 25
Embattled Elites Equivalence and
    Commiseration School, 57–59
"engagement" policy, xii, 26,
    40–41, 104
    of George H. W. Bush, 79–80
equal protection of the law, 20

factory managers, authority of, 16
Falun Gong, 17, 31, 53, 96
fiftieth anniversary of the founding
    of the People's Republic of
    China, 94
Ford, Gerald, administration of,
    74, 77
Fragile Relationship, A (Harding),
    40
Fraser, John, 36
free trade, 26–27, 39
    see also trade with China
Friedman, Thomas, 14, 97

Gates, Bill, 105
globalization, 14, 82
Google, 17, 105
Gorbachev, Mikhail, xi, 25
    visit to China, 95–96
Gore, Al, 3
Greenberg, Maurice (Hank),
    62–63
Guangdong, 12

Haass, Richard, 13, 103
Harding, Harry, 40
"hedged integration," 40, 41
Heritage Foundation, xi, 62, 63
Hills, Carla A., 60
Hills & Co., 60
Hong Kong, xi, 12, 94
Hu Jintao, 16, 22, 24, 32, 87
human rights in China, 34, 38, 111
    George H. W. Bush and, 77
    Carter and, 18, 74–75
    Clinton and, 69, 80–84
    linking trade and, 69, 81, 84,
        103–4, 109
    presidential rationalizations for
        ignoring, 75–76, 80–81
    Reagan and, 76, 77
Hundred Flowers campaign of
    1956–1957, 36
Hungary, 78

India, 70, 76
Indonesia, 76
integration, strategy of, xii, 103–9
intellectual property rights, 65
International Republican Institute,
    18
Internet in China, 3, 16–18,
    58–59, 63, 105
Iran, 86
Iran, shah of, 75
Iraq war, 38, 85

Japan, 59, 76, 79, 80
Japan bashing, 30–31
Jiang Yanyong, 16
Jiang Zemin, 2, 16, 24, 94
judiciary in China, 21, 107

Kamm, John, 34
Kantor, Mickey, 60–61
Karimov, Islam, 24–25
Khrushchev, Nikita, 73

Kissinger, Henry, 42, 61, 72, 74,
    77
  China policy, 33, 41, 70
  consulting firm, 60
  personal relationship with
    Chinese leadership, 34, 71,
    72
Kissinger Associates, 60
Kristof, Nicholas D., 49, 50

Lampton, David M., 40, 58
Lee Teng-hui, 35
legal system, Chinese, 21, 107
Lexus and the Olive Tree, The
    (Friedman), 14
Lieberthal, Kenneth, 61
Lord, Winston, 77

McCarthyism, 41, 42, 43
MacLaine, Shirley, 55
Mao Zedong, 41, 44, 52, 55, 72
  Nixon's 1972 meeting with, 6, 9
Mayer, Brown, Rowe and Maw, 61
Microsoft, 17, 105
middle class, Chinese, 50, 107–8
  democratization of China and,
    51–52, 53
  as proportion of China's
    population, 51–52
  support for the status quo,
    53–54, 66–67, 108
  visitors' contact with, 55–57
Mitchell, George, 81, 111
most-favored-nation trade status,
    26, 33
Mugabe, Robert, 24, 25
multinational corporations, see
    business and financial
    interests in China

NAFTA (North American Free
    Trade Agreement), 26, 82
National Democratic Institute, 18
National Interest, 62

nationalism, Chinese, 59
Nationalist China, 12, 41, 56, 63,
    72–73, 97–98
National People's Congress, 16, 99
National Security Council, x, 70
neoconservatives, 38, 85
New York Times, 5, 31
Nixon, Richard, administration of
  China policy, 26, 33, 34, 41, 42,
    70, 72–74
  Indo-Pakistan war and, 70
  "kitchen debate" with
    Khrushchev, 73
  Mao Zedong and, 6, 9
Nixon Center, 62
nongovernmental agencies, 4
"nonstate actors," 101
North Korea, 86, 101
Nye, Joseph, 38

Olympics Games of 2008, Beijing
    summer, 89–100
  China's domestic TV coverage
    of, 93–95
  clichéd images of China, 89–91
  emergence of China as world
    power and, 89
  media coverage of, 89–95
  visitors to China, 96–100
one-party system in China
  authoritarian regimes supported
    by, 24–25, 105–6
  Beijing Olympics of 2008,
    domestic TV coverage of,
    93–95
  middle-class support for, 53–54,
    66–67
  the people of China,
    implications for, 23–24,
    36–37, 44–45, 108
  persistence of, xiii, 7, 102,
    105–7
  resolution of disputes within the
    party, 24, 59

suppression of dissent, *see*
dissent in China, suppression
of

Third Scenario and, *see* Third
Scenario

Tiananmen crackdown, *see*
Tiananmen crackdown

transfer of power, 24

Upheaval Scenario, 7–10

village elections and, 18–20,
106–7

visitors to China and skewed
information, 54–56

see also political liberalization
of China

Pakistan, 70

"panda huggers," 46, 47

patriotism, Chinese, 93, 94–95

Pelosi, Nancy, 81, 111

Pentagon, *see* Defense
Department, U.S.

People's Armed Police, 11, 63

People's Daily, 11

People's Liberation Army, 1, 11,
13, 59, 85

as military threat, 21–23, 37–38,
101–2

Tiananmen crackdown and, *see*
Tiananmen crackdown

Philippines, 44, 76

Poland, 78

political liberalization of China,
13–18, 44–45, 49–67, 98–100

Beijing Olympics and, 99–100

business interests and, *see*
business and financial
interests in China

freedom of speech, 15–18, 65,
105

freedom of the press, 14, 16

the Internet and, 16–18

mistake is assuming the future,
102

people of China and, 23–24,
36–37, 44–45

P-factor, 69–88

reexamination of U.S. policy,
110–12

rule of law, 18, 20–21, 98, 107

Soothing Scenario, *see*
Soothing Scenario

strategy of integration, 103–5

Third Scenario and, *see* Third
Scenario

Tiananmen crackdown, *see*
Tiananmen crackdown

timing of, 108–9

trade and, xiii, 2, 3, 26–27, 45,
46, 103, 110

U.S. "engagement" policy and,
see "engagement" policy

village elections, 18–20, 106–7

see also economic liberalization
in China; one-party system in
China

political prisoners, 3–5, 6, 16

"quiet diplomacy" and, 5

Pomfret, John, 94

Powell, Colin, 33

press, freedom of the, 14, 16

"provocative" epithet, xii, 34–36

"pushing the envelope," 35

Putin, Vladimir, 25

Reagan, Ronald, administration
of, 13, 76–77

Republican Party, 18

Rice, Condoleezza, 104

rich and poor, disparity between
China's, 7, 8

Roosevelt, Franklin D.,
administration of, 97–98

Roosevelt, Theodore, 9

rule of law, 18, 20–21, 98, 107

Rumsfeld, Donald, 32, 85

rural-urban divide in China,
51–53, 55, 56–57

Samuelson, Robert J., 37
San Francisco Chronicle, 34
SARS disease in China, 16
Saudi Arabia, 25
scenarios for China's future, *see*
    Soothing Scenario; Third
    Scenario; Upheaval Scenario
Schell, Orville, 55
Scowcroft, Brent, 60, 77, 79
Segal, Gerald, 8
September 11 attacks, 85, 101
Shanghai, 12
Somoza, Anastasio, 75
Soothing Scenario, 1–7, 11–12,
    45–46, 83, 87, 110, 112
  American politicians and, 2–5,
    6, 83–84, 87–88
  Beijing 2008 Olympic Games
    and, 92–93
  explanations for repression in
    China, 4, 5–6
  as mainstream American view, 2
  other East Asian countries and,
    12–13, 44, 50–51, 87
  rule of law, 18, 20–21, 98
  village elections and, 18–20,
    106–7
South Africa, 79
South Korea, 76
  economic liberalization and
    democracy in, 12–13, 44, 51,
    87
Soviet Union, 12, 23, 64, 75
  cold war and U.S. China policy,
    26, 32–33, 77, 78, 82, 102
  Reagan administration and, 76,
    77
speech, freedom of, 15–18, 65, 105
  see also dissent in China,
    suppression of
Starr, Cornelius V., 62
State Department, U.S., x, 34, 61,
    70
  China hands and, 42–43

Stonebridge International, 60,
    61
strategic dialogue, 33
strategy of integration, xii, 103–9
Sudan, 25
Syria, 25, 86

Taiwan, 33–34, 35, 72–73, 76
  Carter China policy, 71
  economic liberalization and
    democracy in, 12–13, 51,
    87
  U.S. arms sales to, 69, 79
television coverage of Beijing
    Olympic Games of 2008,
    93–95
terrorism, 101
think tanks, x, xi, 61–63
Third Scenario, 10–13, 95, 112
  implications for the U.S.,
    21–27, 105–8
Tiananmen crackdown, xi, 6, 14,
    16, 17, 36, 44, 78, 95–96, 109
  China's economic vulnerability
    after, 80, 109
Tibetan activists, 3, 96
tourists, *see* visitors to China
trade with China, xiii, 32, 33, 62,
    81–84
  linkage of human rights and,
    69, 81–82, 83, 103–4, 109
  political liberalization argument
    for, xiii, 2, 26–27, 45, 46, 84,
    103, 110
  reexamination of U.S. policy, 111
  strategy of integration, 103–4,
    109
  U.S. trade deficit, 84
"troublemakers," 35
Two Steps Forward, One Step
    Back approach, 5

Uighur activists, 3, 96
unemployment in the U.S., 26, 108

United Nations Human Rights
    Commission, 83, 99
United Nations Security Council,
    85
U.S. China policy
    consistency of, since Nixon
        administration, 40–41
    historically, *see names of*
        individual presidential
        administrations
Upheaval Scenario, 7–10, 112
    Beijing Olympics of 2008 and,
        95–96
urban-rural divide in China,
    51–53, 55, 56–57
Uzbekistan, 24–25

village elections, 18–20, 106–7
visitors to China, 96–100
    Beijing Olympics of 2008 and,
        96, 99

skewed impressions of, 54–57,
    98–100

wages in China, 66
Washington Post, 33–34, 46, 47, 94
Wei Jingsheng, 75
Wherry, Kenneth, 12
WilmerHale, 61
World Bank, 80
World Trade Organization
    (WTO), China's membership
    in, 26–27, 32, 61, 83, 103, 109

Yahoo!, 17, 105
Yang Jiechi, 85
Yeltsin, Boris, 25

Zhao Ziyang, 3, 16
Zhou Enlai, 71, 72
Zimbabwe, 24, 25, 86, 105
Zoellick, Robert, 104

Rise of the Vulcans:
The History of Bush's War Cabinet

When George W. Bush campaigned for the White House, he was such a novice in foreign policy that he couldn't name the president of Pakistan and momentarily suggested he thought the Taliban was a rock and roll band. But he relied upon a group called the Vulcans—an inner circle of advisers with a long, shared experience in government, dating back to the Nixon, Ford, Reagan, and first Bush administrations. After returning to power in 2001, the Vulcans were at first expected to restore U.S. foreign policy to what it had been under George H. W. Bush and previous Republican administrations. Instead, the Vulcans put America on an entirely new and different course, adopting a far-reaching set of ideas that attempted to change the world and America's role in it. *Rise of the Vulcans* is nothing less than a detailed, incisive thirty-five-year history of the top six members of the Vulcans—Dick Cheney, Donald Rumsfeld, Colin Powell, Paul Wolfowitz, Richard Armitage, and Condoleezza Rice—and their roles in the era of unilateral American military power.

"An astute group biography." —*The New York Times Book Review*

ISBN 978-0-14-303489-6